PARENTS AS TALENT DEVELOPERS

ESSENTIAL PARENTING TOOLS OF EXCEPTIONAL PARENTS

JAMES REED CAMPBELL

BRENDA HAREWOOD

authorHOUSE®

AuthorHouse™
1663 Liberty Drive
Bloomington, IN 47403
www.authorhouse.com
Phone: 1 (800) 839-8640

Published by AuthorHouse   01/26/2017

ISBN: 978-1-5246-5509-9 (sc)
ISBN: 978-1-5246-5510-5 (hc)
ISBN: 978-1-5246-5508-2 (e)

Library of Congress Control Number: 2016920978

Print information available on the last page.

Any people depicted in stock imagery provided by Thinkstock are models, and such images are being used for illustrative purposes only. Certain stock imagery © Thinkstock.

This book is printed on acid-free paper.

CHAPTER 1

How Parental Influence Works

Knowledge is the prime need of the hour.

Mary McLeod Bethune, Educator

Introduction

The structure of this book is designed to provide an easy resource to read and share with extended family members. Our goal is to empower parents and extended family by giving you tools, strategies, and game plans needed to help your children become high achievers in school. By helping your children be more productive during their formative years in school, you will provide a solid basis for high achievement in adulthood.

Parents will always be the essential link between the child and a successful school experience. In the minority community, this is especially true. The support and involvement of the minority family is one of the most significant factors in determining student academic success.

The book provides ninety-two practical ideas, which we call "kernels." This is a technical term used in therapy and medical fields to classify practices that work. Kernels are seeds in the plant world. The kernels on an ear of corn are the seeds needed to grow the next generation of corn. We use this term in the sense that each parental practice we highlight in this book should be viewed as a seed for your child's academic growth. It needs to be nourished and cultivated in order to grow and prosper.

How did we find the kernels that are contained in this book? Our research teams went to public schools in minority neighborhoods in New York City and Long Island to find high-achieving African American and Latino children. We then visited their families and interviewed the parents and their children separately to uncover what they did to warrant such high achievement.

These *exceptional parents,* as we refer to them, took the initiative in working with their children, expressed their expectations openly, and followed through with the necessary behavior and support to ensure their children performed well and gained the sense that they could really "make it" in school. *It is these minority parents who are the instructors in this book.* We have talked with them, written down their stories, and extracted the practices they used.

These kernels are embedded in various chapters, where they are explained in detail. They are also summarized in the appendix to help you focus your attention on them. We recommend photocopying the list of kernels and keeping them easily available to remind you of your possible courses of action. Post them on your refrigerator. Place a copy in your day planner. Staple a copy onto your child's chore chart. Frequently referring to the kernels will help you pick and choose among them as you construct the particular course of action for your child.

Some of the kernels listed in this book are things educators consider basic, for example, *"Structure everything for education first,"* and *"Homework must be completed every day."* Many kernels are messages you can deliver to your children. For example, *"Education gives you life skills,"* and *"Ability without effort goes nowhere."* Other kernels are how-to approaches, such as *"Ask your child what he or she learned in school today,"* or *"Examine the TV listings; lay out the TV programs for the week, selecting the worthwhile programs."* Other kernels listed at the ends of different chapters are specific dos and don'ts. They clearly define what an acceptable behavior is and what behaviors should be avoided.

Kernels are easy to use.
Kernels help organize the learning process.
Kernels can contribute to motivation.
Kernels contain no professional jargon.
Kernels are microlevel things that effective parents use.

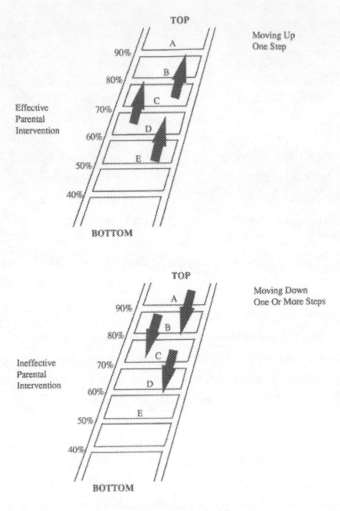

Figure 1.1. Grade ladders.

Your Child's Potential

In 1962 Wilbur Brookover, a prominent American sociologist, advanced the idea that most human beings use only 20 percent of their mental capacity. We are born with much more natural ability than we ever use. His hope was that during the next decades, researchers would uncover ways to help people use more and more of their potential.

Our purpose in writing this book is to help African American and Latino parents provide the best possible growing conditions for their children's development so that more than 20 percent of their capacity is developed. Parents can either provide the best possible environment for growth and development at one extreme, or at the other extreme, neglect their obligations and leave their children's development to chance.

One way to understand the effects of a parent's influence is summarized in the two grade ladders illustrated in figure 1.1. Each rung in the ladder represents a 10 percent increase from the rung below. We have labeled the top rungs with the letter grades A, B, C, and so on. A parent's efforts can move his or her child up one or two steps.

If parents completely neglect their obligations, they can negatively affect their children's achievement. For example, some parents won't accept the responsibility that goes with being a parent. They have no interest in their children and resent child-rearing obligations. Neglectful wealthy parents ship their children off to boarding schools and thus buy their own freedom. Minority neglectful parents put as little into their involvement as possible. Their neglect is responsible for moving their children down the ladder by any number of rungs.

The child, however, is also part of the equation. Children see these instances of neglect. How do you think they feel about these experiences? How does the neglect affect their self-esteem? It must be remembered that a child's motivation is necessary for any work done in school.

Which Parental Involvement Works Best?

Let us provide an overview on optimal parental involvement. Later in the book we will be more specific. The successful parents in our research studies created an emphasis on learning from the very beginning of their children's lives. They realized the need to develop their children's talents. They did not wait for the schools or for professional educators to do this job.

To accomplish this goal, they tried to supply as many stimuli to their children's development as early and as often as possible. This included promoting early literacy, talking to the child as often as possible early in the child's life, and taking him or her to places in their communities that would stimulate the child. These activities show your children you are interested in them. When children see parents putting in substantial amounts of time with them, they see the parents' commitment with their own eyes.

Part of this development is to nurture the right attitudes and values. Successful parents also want to get their children to build a work ethic that will endure. This includes carefully monitoring the children's early schoolwork in the beginning and then gradually disengaging in order to encourage them to assume responsibility. The parents teach their children to avoid distractions that would lead them away from what is important to their learning. They guide their children to make friendships with other children from responsible families that share their values, and they monitor their children's peers so that those academically inclined are encouraged and those with poor attitudes and values are discouraged.

The ideal is to make sure that your children are comfortable in any situation where learning is taking place, where their talents can be developed, and to recognize and appreciate adults that can help develop their talents.

Academic Home Climate

Before introducing the academic home climate, let us describe what we mean by *climate*. It refers to the way your home is organized. A sports climate means that the TV is frequently tuned to sporting events. The family always reads the sports sections in newspapers. Children in such homes feel comfortable dealing with people where sports are central.

Academic refers to *learning*, and the climate again refers to how your home is organized. These homes provide the resources needed for learning new things. In such a climate, it is natural for children to learn.

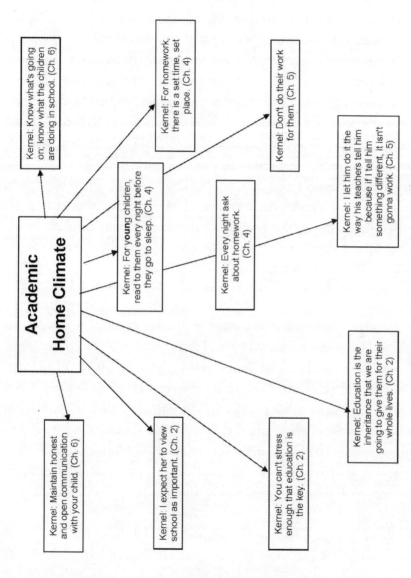

Figure 1.2. Academic home climate.

Figure 1.2 shows the big picture, with the *academic home climate* as the organizing principle. The kernels are from several chapters and constitute the microlevel. Think of the *academic home climate* as a hothouse for learning and development, where talents can be identified and then nurtured. Successful parents create and sustain such a climate. In our studies we uncovered hundreds of specific practices that parents use to organize the learning process, to provide the needed motivation, and to assure that their children will succeed in school. Since all of the kernels concern learning or school-related things, we believe the kernels are essentially academic in nature. Children prosper when they find that their school has the same academic climate that exists in their homes.

Children feel comfortable in familiar surroundings where they know what to expect and how to act. This comfort gives them more confidence to work with their teachers. The more closely you can mesh these climates, the more advantages you will give your children.

Academic Home Climate Generates Positive Payoffs

Our research studies put us in contact with many children whose parents established *academic home climates*. Homes that establish this climate upgrade their children's academic productivity by 20 to 30 percent. As mentioned above, this means moving up the grade ladder. When these climates exist, what payoffs are generated? Table 1.1 summarizes the behaviors we observed from children being raised in such climates. Our recommendation to parents is to make these nineteen payoffs their ultimate goals. No parent can accomplish all of these payoffs overnight. However, with persistent application, these goals can be achieved.

Ability to Accept Challenges: Parents should help children see that many hurdles in life should be seen as challenges, not towering or unattainable barriers. When children find school subjects to be difficult and get low or failing grades, they should view these experiences as wake-up calls to put in more effort. Failure can be changed when it is analyzed and diagnosed as a learning experience.

Adaptability: Adaptability is a great skill to nurture in a child. Teaching your children to use their abilities and talents to solve their own problems is a skill that can be applied over and over again throughout life. It is one of the secrets to many people's success.

Attitudes (in many areas): Positive attitudes are essential to have in many situations in life. Children must learn to have a sense of responsibility about their obligations to their families. They should be taught to adapt and be encouraged to be tolerant. They also need to understand the importance of being reliable.

Attitudes (toward school and the teacher): Since school should be one of the crucial places where learning takes place, children must view it in a positive light. We stated above that children should be taught to view anyone capable of developing their talents with respect and openness. Both school and teachers should be seen as great assets. Both should be presented as great sources of potential for your children's growth.

Attributions (ability): Attributions concern your children's talents and how they handle such talents. Several years ago in his sermon, a priest made the point that all of our talents come as gifts from God. If we have many talents, we should not feel superior in any way because they are gifts. Instead, we owe it to God to develop these talents and use them to help others in society. This message needs to be delivered to your child. Since every child has a myriad of talents, it is up to parents to nurture each child's development. We will provide more information about attributions in chapter 2.

Attributions (effort): Effort attributions refer to the determination your child devotes to his or her school subjects. Again, more information about this topic will be presented in chapter 2.

Beliefs: There are many beliefs that need to be instilled in your children, including the belief that your children can trust the family and the importance of understanding their purpose in life. Ethnic or cultural beliefs are imperative to pass on to the next generation. Another necessary belief is the importance of spirituality. Church attendance every week can help the child understand the greater demands of morality. We do, however, recognize that spirituality is not limited to a particular church or faith.

Cognitive Growth: In the section above, we provided information on how successful parents stimulated their children's development. We present more information about this topic in later chapters.

Curiosity: Encouraging children to develop healthy curiosity is a positive development. In so many walks of life, curiosity is needed to be successful. Investigators in many occupations benefit from being curious. Curiosity lets them pursue leads that solve mysteries and ultimately make them successful. Students also benefit by being curious. It drives them to find out more about things that pique their interest. These probes make them stronger students.

Readiness: Children that do well at school are the ones who have been the best prepared. Teachers call this readiness. Effective parents spend preschool years trying to stimulate their children's thinking. They also get their children ready for school by teaching them many of the beginning things that will be covered in kindergarten and the early grades.

Development of a Work Ethic: This outcome is something that came as a surprise to the research team. We found that our exceptional parents deliberately engineered the development of a work ethic for their children. Learning the value of working to accomplish a desired goal is something that can be developed and nurtured. Using this to overcome challenges can become a great strength that children can carry with them their whole lives.

Expectations/Aspirations: Research shows that parental expectations have positive effects on children's academic achievement. Children that report their parents want them to attend college and eventually become professionals have higher achievement. Parents get this message across by communicating it to their children in many ways. Chapter 2 will present more information about this topic.

Interests: Encouraging their children's natural interests to grow and develop requires parents to spend time observing and deciphering when their children put in time and what they like to do with this time. As a child, the scientist Charles Darwin was fascinated with beetles. He collected and studied them. He became known for his collection. As people found out about his interest, they mailed beetles to him from all over the world. By the time he was a teen, he had one of the largest beetle collections in the world. Obviously, this interest led to his brilliant career in science.

Level of Commitment: Children must realize the drive needed to excel. Parents must recognize the need to get their children to be passionate about learning and excelling.

Motivation: One of the key things that good teachers do is to motivate their students. Parents need to motivate their children because if the children do not see learning as relevant and useful, they will not put in the needed effort. Motivation is much like salesmanship. The goal is to get the child to be self-motivated.

Respect for Authority: Teach children to respect those in authority. As mentioned above, teachers represent the earliest talent developers that a child will meet outside the home. Children need to respect these adults and be attuned to what is being taught. Other authority figures are the local minister and other adults in the community.

Sociability: Teach children to develop viable peer and adult relationships. Effective parents want their children to be able to get along with a diversity of people.

Values: Encourage the value of lifelong learning because in our evolving world, learning new things is no longer just for children. In today's world everyone periodically needs to reinvent themselves. Children also need to be encouraged to be persistent. In addition, morality is something that needs to be constantly brought up.

Ways to Communicate: A substantial number of studies show that children in families with good communication get better achievement. Everything you do with your children should revolve around establishing lines of communication. Families with viable communication linkages avoid many of the problems that plague families with poor lines of communication. We expand this topic more fully in chapter 6.

What Parent Behavior Does Not Work?

Although this book is about what successful African American and Latino parents do, let's examine some research about *what not to do.* Some parents believe that when their children enroll in school, their job of providing an education is finished; in other words, the main responsibility for their child's education is in the hands of the teachers and the school. They are glad to see this responsibility in the hands of professionals.

Some parents investigate neighborhoods that have the best schools and make great economic sacrifices by purchasing expensive homes in these neighborhoods. With this decision they assure themselves that their children will get a quality education.

This was the case for a number of African American parents in the affluent suburb of Shaker Heights, Ohio. This parental expectation was dashed, however, when many of their children ended up in the lowest academic level in these schools. The chance of attending college disappeared. Their subpar high school achievement trashed their families' sacrifices.

The African American parents were so upset that they commissioned Dr. John Ogbu, a famous educational researcher from the University of California at Berkeley, to conduct a study that would explain their children's underachievement. In 2003 Ogbu's research team did an intensive study of the problem and published their results in the book *Black American Students in an Affluent Suburb: A Study of Academic Disengagement.*[1] (We have extracted some kernels from Ogbu's study that you will see in subsequent chapters in this book.)

Even though these well-to-do African American parents occupied positions in the professions, the basic finding of Ogbu's study was that these *African American parents did not provide the parenting that was essential for academic excellence because they were too busy making the money that was needed to live in these high-status communities.*[2] These professional parents assumed that their children understood the need to accumulate the academic credentials needed to enter the same professions, but their seventy-hour workweeks left little time for any personal interaction with their children. Many of them were already at work when the children awoke in the morning and did not return home until late in the evening. Their children were essentially on their own before and after school. Parental neglect undermined their children's motivation. *Moving to communities with the best schools is not enough.*

Parents have only so many hours in the day to connect with their children. This connection must be strong and consistent (daily) to provide the support needed to influence academic achievement. Parents must get more involved if they want their children to have careers in the same types of businesses and professions where they are employed.

Compare the payoffs listed in Table 1.1 with Ogbu's findings. How many of the nineteen payoffs did the Shaker Heights parents get right? Without question, these African American children had all the brainpower needed to do well in these schools. However, they felt neglected and literally jumped off the achievement ladder. They rebelled because they believed their parents were never there for them. They got even for their parents' neglect.

Role Models

All children need role models to emulate as they move through school. The extended family, grandparents, uncles, aunts, and family friends constitute a pool of potential role models. The church congregation represents another source where high-achieving children that are close to your child's age can serve this purpose. Our research indicates that academically oriented peers tend to hang around other successful students; therefore, guiding your child to make friends with such children can pay high dividends. This might also be accomplished by your family becoming friends with the parents of such children. An ideal setting for these contacts is your church's congregation.

Many schools and companies offer on-site mentoring opportunities after school and during the summer months. Some Google offices offer a three-week internship to expose students to hands-on experiences using computer technology. Some high schools sponsor full-day sessions with local business leaders who inform students about the educational path they took to achieve success. Individual students are able to shadow the professionals in the community for a full day. Students report very positive feedback in this real-world career-focused experience.

There is a large pool of successful minority adults that can serve as role models. We begin each of the first eight chapters with inspirational quotes from famous individuals of color. These eight individuals are selected as role models. The Bureau of Labor Statistics reports that in 2012, the percentage of African Americans employed in the high-paying management sector was 11.1 percent and 18.4 percent in the professions sector.[3] For Latinos, the percentages were 8.9 percent and 11.8 percent, respectively.[4] For African Americans, these percentages, when added together, accounted for 4,677,520. For Latinos, the total was 4,528,746. Therefore, in both minority communities, there was a large pool of successful people to serve as role models.

In the same Bureau of Labor Statistics report, data on college attendance showed a total of 12,236,000 African Americans, including 5,136,000 with college or higher degrees.[5] For Latinos the number attending college was 10,188,000, including 4,211,000 with college or higher degrees.[6] These millions of successful people have blazed the trail for the next generation of minority students. Only in America does this continue to happen. We recommend that parents use these statistics to motivate their children.

------------------------Key Ideas------------------------

- Most human beings use only 20 percent of their mental capacity. We are born with much more natural ability than we ever use.
- It is the position of the authors of this book that parents have the potential to upgrade their children's academic output or lower their children's academic output by 20 to 30 percent.
- Conversely, if parents completely neglect their obligations, they can negatively affect their children's achievement. Such influence can cause a child to score lower on the academic ladder than he or she might otherwise.
- Parents influence their children in at least nineteen ways.
- Effective parents establish an *academic home climate* in their homes.
- Achievement is promoted when this climate meshes with the academic climate in the school.
- Moving the family to neighborhoods with good schools is not enough.
- African Americans must use Black college graduates and professionals as role models, rather than professional sports figures.
- There are many highly successful Latinos in every walk of life that can serve as effective role models.

Chapter 1 Notes

1 J. Ogbu. (2003). Black American students in an affluent suburb: A study of academic disengagement. Mahwah, NJ: Lawrence Erlbaum Associates, 2003. 218-249.
2 Ibid.
3 U.S. Bureau of Labor Statistics. "BLS reports Report 1044." Accessed October 2013. 21.
4 Ibid. 21.
5 Ibid. 19.
6 Ibid. 20.

CHAPTER 2

Your Child's Success Starts with Parental Expectations

Be Black, shine, aim high.

Leontyne Price

Translating Parental Expectations

As a parent you know more about the joys, challenges, and demands of life than your child does. You also know more about the various stages of life that your child will experience and what is best for him or her at each stage. How do you blend your own expectations with those derived by your child? Your role as the parent is to expand your child's expectations. It is your belief system that will cause your child to know that the sky is the limit in what he or she can achieve. The one caution we urge parents is to make sure that all expectations originate with the child's natural interests. Don't try to move the child into a career where money is the best, but the child has neither interest nor desire for that field. There are enough financial rewards in professional and managerial careers without overemphasizing those that pay the highest. Wouldn't it be better for a child with a lively interest in bugs to become an entomologist (scientist specializing in insects) than a frustrated, but rich, surgeon? The only way to shape your child's expectations positively is by realizing the importance of talking with and understanding your child, trusting his or her inclinations, supporting his or her goals, and always being your child's greatest supporter.

There are two ways to transmit expectations to your child:

a. *parental conversations*
b. *parental example*

    a. **Parental Conversations:** The first and most important way to gain influence with your children is to realize the importance of conversations that allow them to express their successes, their hopes, and their fears. This also offers an opportunity for the parent to respond and have an input into the way the children think about their experiences. This gives parents the chance to teach and utilize the many kernels that are presented in this chapter. These conversations should involve both quality time and a sufficient quantity of time. As parents of twenty-first-century youth, you will always compete with electronics and varied forms of technology to get your children's attention. Of course, this will be a challenge, but know that social media, which is a very important part of your children's learning and communication with peers, cannot and should not replace the very important one-to-one communication with you. This must be a priority several times a week.

Kernel: **Quality time, simply put, is when your child wants time.**
Kernel: **Quality time is important. Even with a busy schedule, take the time to show him or her that you care.**

Our exceptional parents told us that the optimal time for a child to initiate a conversation is when the child arrives home from school. From scores of interviews with exceptional parents, the vast majority (over 95 percent) have at least one parent or a member of the extended family at home when the child arrives from school. If you can't be home at this optimal time, when you do get home, go directly to your child to get the day's school news. If possible, take your work break at the time your child arrives home from school so that you can begin the conversation on the phone and complete it upon arrival at home.

We recommend that parents put in as much time as possible with their children. It takes time to develop relationships. Remember that your child is a unique personality that needs to be understood, nurtured, and appreciated. It takes time to become sensitive to all the different qualities your child possesses.

    b. ***Parental Example:*** *The way a parent leads his or her life can make a stronger statement to a child than a sea of words.* Parents should be models of the qualities they are trying to instill in their children. You can't urge anyone to listen to your words when your deeds portray just the opposite. If you want your children to restrict their TV viewing, you must also demonstrate the same trait. Similarly, if you smoke cigarettes but forbid your children to smoke, it usually follows that when the children grow older, they, too, will acquire the same smoking habit. "Do as I say, not as I do" will show the parent to be a phony and will demoralize children instead of inspiring them. Parents are powerful role models for children. It goes with the territory; therefore, that parents have a great responsibility to model the qualities that they want their children to develop. It is also important to surround your child with positive role models that you want them to emulate, perhaps beyond the scope of what you have personally achieved. These models or mentors can be former classroom teachers, school administrators, practitioners in the field of interest, clergy, neighbors, relatives, or close family and friends.

Let us examine some of the kernels that exceptional parents use with their children.

What Expectations Do Successful Minority Parents Advocate?

Minority parents should stress the importance of education to their children. All exceptional parents emphasized this point and gave examples of how they transmitted this expectation. Three kernels illustrate their views.

Kernel: **Education is the key to a successful life.**

Kernel: **My son knows how I feel about education because I am like a broken record every time I remind him that our ancestors fought and died for the right to go to school and to get a good education.**

Kernel: **I expect my child to view school as important.**

These parents insist that their children take school seriously. They believe in education and view it as a necessary foundation for their children's future. They realize their children will need to build a future on this footing. The message below is one that children need to understand all through their school careers.

Kernel: Without education you can't go anywhere.

One mother with a number of young and older children told us to "keep talking to your children about the importance of education regardless of how old they are." She keeps insisting on the importance of getting a good education for her children at every level of school.

Kernel: Education is what matters.

Expecting Your Child to Realize His or Her Potential

Exceptional parents maximize their children's talents. They want to develop their children's capabilities. These parents emphasize "being the best you can be" to their children.

Kernel: I just want my children to realize their potential and not to be afraid of it.

Our research with minority families uncovered many interesting stories about the persistence of different family members in getting educated despite many substantial obstacles. Two of the families answered our questions by providing motivational stories they derived from past generations. One mother came from a sharecropping Virginia family that scratched out a living by requiring every able-bodied family member to work in the fields. This is the story they tell to succeeding generations of children: "Grandmother was required to work on the farm unless there was a test at school. She told her father she had different tests frequently enough so that eventually she was able to graduate from high school." Grandmother certainly had the *grit and determination* to rise above the meager life that awaited sharecroppers' children in that era. She realized that getting an education was a way to better herself and, in the long run, benefit her own children and even inspire her grandchildren.

There are lots of generational stories that are used to motivate children. These stories give some context about living conditions that their parents and grandparents experienced and the difficulties they faced. Such stories are excellent ways to connect the generations.

Another mother tells this story: "Your grandmother stood on her feet for eight hours straight so that we could have a roof over our heads and food to eat. Is that what you want for yourself?"

Kernel: Education is food for the mind.

Within many of these successful minority families, grandmothers assume significant roles. They make themselves available for "duty" when the family needs them and are a good source of psychological support for their grandchildren. Consequently, the important role grandmothers play appears in quite a few kernels. One grandmother explained that education has the potential to give children skills they can use over a lifetime.

Kernel: Education gives you life skills.

A grandfather in a Latino family saw education as a way to "break the chain" of poverty that shackled the family for generations.

Kernel: We have to do handwork to make hard money. If our child gets an education, he or she will get that opportunity. That will be like breaking the chain, and that will benefit my pride. I'd be proud of my children if they became construction workers, but I would love for them to get a little piece of paper that says they're a "this."

This grandfather looked upon the education of his grandchild as a unique opportunity for the family. He was proud of his grandchild and wanted him to go beyond the menial labor (handwork) that supported their family with low wages (hard money). In the United States, construction workers can make decent salaries, but he wanted his child to get a college or professional degree ("a this"). He wanted this child to break the chain for the whole family.

Kernel: **Value education by saying it so often that your child believes it.**

Many of these minority parents urge their children to be the best they can be. This is a consistent message they funnel to their children. It begins at birth at the naming of the child. One mother established expectations by selecting the African name Kamilika (Swahili), which specified the qualities she wanted her son to emulate. *Kamilika* means "to be complete; to strive for excellence." This name gave him an African context to be proud of and a formula for self-actualization.

Lifelong Expectations

Kernel: **Whatever you are, you must be the best at it.**

The expectations described above mostly deal with school and grades, but many of these parents are looking further ahead. They are thinking about possible careers or the possibility that their child can accomplish something significant. One mother told us "set high expectations—perhaps my daughter will be a writer and illustrator, like this trio: Patricia Palocco (*January's Sparrow*), Eric Carle (*The Very Hungry Caterpillar*), or Jeanette Winter (*Follow the Drinking Gourd).*" These publications are widely used in today's schools.

However, there are also famous minority authors to emulate, such as Gabriel Garcia Marquez and Carlos Fuentes (Latin America), and equally well-known African American authors like Toni Morrison, Maya Angelou, and Teri Woods.

These parents were preparing their children for college and the professions beyond. One parent described her strategy as follows: "Ever since she was a little girl, I put it in her head that she would be going to college." She casually planted this idea over and over again during the child's early years. After a while the girl visualized her eventual college years as part of her growing up to become a functioning and productive adult. Another parent told us that as a result of her daily conversations during the elementary school years about the value of college, her children began to see college as a natural extension following high school. Again, expectations are established as natural events that follow in the long road to adulthood.

The first kernel listed below is the product of a Latino father, but this one has been used by Jewish, Irish, and German working-class families of past generations. The author, Pete Hamill, still remembers the groans of pain each night from his immigrant father who worked as a day laborer. This searing experience demonstrated the sacrifices being made for him and motivated him to do well.

The second kernel in the pair below has the same message and originates from a hardworking immigrant mother employed in a menial, low-paying job.

Kernel: **He knows that we work so that he can have a better life.**
Kernel: **I want my daughter to be more than I am.**

We interviewed two Latino immigrant families that saw the education they were stressing for their children as an "inheritance." One mother expressed it this way: "Your inheritance is the money we provided to give you the best education. We have nothing more to give." Another saw the sacrifices the family made as the only inheritance they could give to their children. Both families realized they would never be able to provide any financial inheritance.

Kernel: **Education is the inheritance that we are going to give them for their whole lives.**

Another parent paints a realistic picture for her daughter by stressing things that stand in her way for a Black woman. "I want my daughter to achieve, to be successful, and to not let life's circumstances stand in the way of her education, which is ultimately the road to success."

The next kernel serves as a motto for any aspiring family. It is especially useful for many immigrant families that come from humble beginnings. It is one that makes a powerful statement.

Kernel: **It's not where you come from; it's where you are going.**

Only in America could this kernel hold true. The message below is another useful one to use with children. It is short and concise.

Kernel: **Education is the ticket to the future.**

Effort and Ability

Look back to your days in school. When you did well, was it because of your natural ability, or did you have to work hard to achieve something? The same question comes up with every challenge you face in your life today. How do children answer these questions? Children think about the amount of time their friends put in to be successful in a particular subject. Is success due to just being naturally smart? Or is success due to hard work? Each child also views his or her setbacks in the same way. Children who decide they do not have the needed ability simply stop working. Why work when you don't have enough ability in a subject? This defeatist strategy can undermine a child's success and lower his or her expectations.

Other children get suckered into projecting an image of being cool or smart where they really do not have to exert that much effort. They worry more about what others think of them. "Do they think I am talented? If I show that I can only succeed if I put in large amounts of work, does this diminish my image?" The child figures it is better to put in little effort and preserve the desired image. Even if such a child does poorly, everyone will know it is because he or she did not care. In this way the child preserves his or her image.

In our research studies we asked this ability/effort question to the exceptional parents because we wanted to see their role in these areas. *Eighty percent told us that **effort** is the key to school success.* They emphasized that a lack of effort was the reason for many of the failures their children experienced. Here is are some of the kernels that parents gave us.

Kernel: **Effort is necessary for ability to show.**
Kernel: **Ability without effort goes nowhere.**
Kernel: **Ability is what God gave you; effort makes you grow.**
Kernel: **Achievement depends upon effort.**

Very few of these parents saw high ability as the key to success in school. They realized the connection between hard work and achievement. A high level of ability without substantial amounts of effort is a blueprint for frustration and eventually poor performance.

You will have to find out what your children think about these two key concepts: effort and ability. It's important to convince them that smart kids don't have a monopoly on high grades. In fact, when smart children get bored with school, they put in very little effort, and their grades eventually tumble.

The exceptional parents understood the connection between hard work and report card grades. They expected their children to get good grades, and they did the things that were needed to make sure their children put in the needed effort. One parent told us that "I want my child to get the best education possible, and I want to instill in him at an early age how vital it is for him to do well in school." This parent realized that it was necessary to make sure that her expectations for him were established in the early grades and that her child worked up to his potential.

The kernel listed below originated from a Latino immigrant family, but our research teams have found the same kernel being used by Asian American, Jewish, and African American families.

Kernel: **If there are children that get one hundred, my child has to get one hundred.**

This kernel can be controversial because it may appear that too much pressure is being placed on the child. But over the years, many successful professionals told us that their parents communicated the same kernel to them when they were growing up. We include it in this book because it works! Parents that use this kernel notch up their expectations—*don't be satisfied when you have the ability to do better*. This message also makes the connection that more effort will result in even higher grades and more satisfaction.

These parents recognize that children need to do work in order to do well. One parent told us that she expects her child to extend herself well beyond school hours. She makes sure that her children do their homework and studying at home.

Another parent advised talking about the relevance of effort to success. She wants her child to realize that getting good grades is not just due to good luck. Children sometimes feel that success is simply due to chance. They may think they can only do well when they have a caring teacher who explains the material clearly, but sometimes they may have poor teachers who do not like them. Sometimes they may study the wrong material, material that does not appear on the test. All of these things can be considered bad luck. Still, children must learn that with the right amount of effort, they can do well despite these difficulties.

The particular experience of minorities doing well came through in our interviews with these exceptional parents. One parent commented, "Life is hard for us, but it was harder for our ancestors. In comparison, our lives are much better; at least we can go to school. And if we can get in the door to better opportunities, which is cracked open for us, we are walking in on the shoulders and the tears of those who came before us." This parent wants her child to appreciate the difficulties that previous generations experienced in trying to better themselves. She wants to get the idea across that the door of opportunity is finally open—but just a little bit. Now is the time to get your foot into that doorway before it is again slammed shut.

The next kernel represents the complete package of qualities that epitomizes the productive and successful adult.

Kernel: **Success is based upon the foundation of hard work, honesty, flexibility, dependability, adaptability, being well-read, and being well-spoken.**

Children must be taught that good things happen when you are committed. It is only with commitment that the drive to excel is possible. You have to devote all of your energy to accomplishing your goal. You often hear the expression "Things are never easy." This expression refers to the fact that difficult goals require commitment. Hurdles always seem to emerge out of nowhere to make things difficult.

Kernel: **If you want good, your nose has to run.**

This message came from a grandmother and deals with making a commitment to doing something important. She was a girl from a sharecropper family in the rural south. What she meant by *your nose has to run* is that in the cotton fields, you couldn't stop for anything. You had to work with such abandon that your nose would sometimes run, but you had to keep going. It contains a gem of wisdom that applies not just to children but to everyone. Everyone has personal liabilities, and all of us experience setbacks. Many of these things are beyond our control. However, instead of feeling sorry for ourselves, we should look for ways to turn the situation around. The successful person learns how to turn negatives into positives. For example, J. K. Rowling, the author of the Harry Potter series of books and movies, faced uniform rejection of her book proposals over a seven-year period. During these years her mother died, and she got divorced and descended into poverty before finally getting her first book published. Several celebrated African American personalities had similar rags to riches stories. One of them, Oprah Gail Winfrey, was born into poverty on a farm in Mississippi in 1954. Yet despite these humble beginnings, she emerged as a successful actress, playwright, producer, and world-famous TV personality.

Kernel: **Make your liability your asset.**

Work or School?

The question posed above is whether to encourage children to work during their school years or to devote all their time to schoolwork. Asian American parents discourage jobs during the school years. Instead, children are urged to put all their energy into schoolwork. Many American parents encourage early work experience because they feel that it leads to the development of independence. It also teaches children the responsibilities of the workplace and the value of money. Parents, however, should keep a watchful eye on such work experiences. The child's primary job is *schooling*. Work should not be allowed to interfere with this primary obligation. Children may neglect their schoolwork to earn money to buy trivial items, such as electronic devices, clothing, shoes, makeup, and so on. Consequently, jobs may place an overemphasis on materialistic goals and undermine the child's long-range future. Parents should step in when children get their priorities out of line.

Kernel: **Your job is school.**

Endpoint

Of the many kernels presented in this chapter, two of them struck us forcefully as pearls of wisdom. The first, a parent's description of a successful person, is comprehensive and hits home like a sledgehammer. The other kernel succinctly summarizes the immigrant experience for generations of Americans.

Pearls of Wisdom

Success is based upon the foundation of hard work, honesty, flexibility, dependability, adaptability, being well-read, and being well-spoken.	It's not where you come from; it's where you are going.

We will end all of the chapters from here forward with a series of do and don't statements that are especially important for parents in the journey of developing a strong work ethic and study habits in their children. The do statements emphasize essential ideas, and we hope that you will strive to eliminate the don'ts from your parenting.

Do	Don't
Please help your child to be self-motivated.	Please don't let your child just do enough to get by.

------------------------Key Ideas-------------------------

- The vast majority of exceptional parents (over 95 percent) arranged to have at least one parent or member of the extended family home when the child arrives from school.
- Minority parents stressed the importance of education and transferred their expectations to their children in a number of ways.
- Children need to learn to sacrifice and to be disciplined in their efforts.
- Parental expectations are instrumental for their children to actualize their potential.
- Minority parents provided stories of previous generations to motivate their children.
- Grandmothers in the minority community exert an important influence on children.
- Exceptional parents strive to develop expectations for lifelong learning.
- Help convince your child that:
  - ✓ Effort is necessary for ability to show.
  - ✓ Ability without effort goes nowhere.
  - ✓ Ability is what God gave you; effort makes you grow.
  - ✓ Achievement depends upon effort.
- The child's primary job is schooling. After-school jobs should not be allowed to interfere with this primary obligation.

CHAPTER 3

Myths That Undermine Commitment

Parents have to parent; the children can't achieve unless we raise expectations, turn off the television sets, and eradicate the slander that says a Black youth with a book is acting White.

President Barack Obama

What is a myth? Webster defines the term to mean "An ill-founded belief held uncritically ... by an interested group." We extracted the myths below from children at many different grade levels. The purpose of this chapter is to inform parents about some common myths that undermine children's motivation. In all cases these myths represent judgments that children make that have never been subjected to any critical analysis.

Commitment-Deflating Myths

1. Acting White is selling out.[1]
2. You'll do as well or as poorly as your friends.
3. Being successful is not cool.
4. Some low-achieving children want to drag their friends down to their level (misery loves company).
5. Smart kids don't have to work hard. (If you do have to work hard, then you are not really smart enough.)

6. There is something wrong with you if you work harder than everyone else.

MYTH Busting

Myth 1. *Acting White is selling out.*

In President Obama's quote at the beginning of this chapter, the term "acting White" refers to the negative peer pressure among Black students in racially mixed schools. This pressure discourages Black students from excelling. Signithia Fordham and John Ogbu coined the term in 1986.[2] They found that many African American children believed this myth. These children were angry at a dominant society they felt was always putting them down. Ogbu found that peer pressure among African American students was negative toward working hard in school.[3] These children interpreted the school curriculum and the White students' use of Standard English as White impositions. Some African American students taunted other Black students who worked hard and called them "Oreos" (Black on the outside, White on the inside). These children were struggling to find their racial identity.

In the Ogbu study, Black children preferred to identify more with the ghetto Black culture than with the high-achieving culture of their parents. These kids were looking for stereotypes that could define them, not the stereotypes personified by their parents. This is diametrically the opposite of what their parents wanted. These parents expected their children to appreciate the struggles needed to secure professional jobs. However, their children saw their identification with ghetto Black culture as a measure of authenticity.

In the last chapter we talked about parents that neglected the responsibilities of establishing relationships with their offspring. The Shaker Heights Black parents expected and assumed that their children would give them some slack because of the demands of their jobs. After all, the affluence alone should have made up for their frequent absences. Their children, however, did not accept their excuses and instead were angry about the neglect. They saw the parents as phonies, and therefore not authentic. In rebellion they contradicted the parents' messages and pleas and instead embraced the ghetto mentality.

Our message to minority parents is to avoid the mistakes of the Shaker Heights **parents. Go in the opposite direction and make it your mission to establish as close a relationship as possible with your child.** This means constantly showing your child how committed you are to his or her welfare.

Myths 2–4. *2. You'll do as well or as poorly as your friends. 3. Being successful is not cool. 4. Some low-achieving children want to drag their friends down to their level (misery loves company).*

These myths illustrate the ways that peers can gut your children's expectations. Children that buy into these myths use popularity as their excuse to dumb down their talents, but this is a ticket to nowhere. As parents, you need to understand how peer pressure can influence your children's behavior. You should be aware of the potential damage that bad companions can do.

Peer Culture vs. Family Culture

There is a strong peer culture in the United States that is not present in other countries where we conducted our studies. This culture competes with your family culture for your children's attention and allegiance and can have positive or negative influences. This peer culture develops during the early school years and blossoms by middle school.

At the positive extreme, children are encouraged to develop self-discipline as a result of their sports, music, art, or drama training, joining the serious academic students to represent the most productive segment of school society. They are the star athletes, the musical soloists or drama performers, and school newspaper writers or editors. Many of them enroll in advanced courses, become part of the school support staff, and sign up for internships in their community. They are busy assembling resumes that will get them into the best colleges. They are on a solid career path to productive careers.

The negative peer culture operates at the other extreme. Instead of participating in school activities that require self-discipline, these children drift into crowds with low expectations, where there are possibilities for alcohol or drug abuse and unwanted pregnancies.

Most children are in the middle between the two extremes. One of your goals as parents is to steer your children into the productive culture and away from the negative one. The stronger your family, the less possibility your child will embrace the negative crowd.

It is for this reason that many of our African American and Latino exceptional parents pay careful attention to their children's peers. As children grow up, they should be more influenced by their families' influence than by peer culture. The *acting White* myth illustrates the negative effects that peer culture can have. That is why so many of our parents supplied us with information about peers. The kernel below was mentioned by five of the African American parents and two of the Latino parents.

Kernel: Have your children bring their friends home; know their friends.

These parents encourage their children to invite friends home so that the parents can make their own judgments about the children's friends. An African American parent goes a step further with the following kernel:

Kernel: **Let your house be the home that your children's friends all gather at because, if you know their friends, it reveals something very important about your own children.**

Several of our exceptional parents recommended meeting socially with the parents of their children's peers. In this way you get to see the values that are being instilled.

Kernel: **Get to know your children's friends' parents.**

Another parent told us to use the children's social media to uncover their friends.

Kernel: **Look at your children's buddy list on the computer. Know what they are doing and with whom they are chatting.**

Myths 5 and 6.   *5. Smart kids don't have to work hard. (If you do have to work hard, then you are not really smart enough.) 6. There is something wrong with you if you work harder than everyone else.*

In the last chapter we contrasted effort and ability. Here we examine the excuses children use to avoid working hard with their schoolwork.

These myths concern the development of a child's work ethic. Children learn about work ethics by observing people around them. Some families own a small business, such as a restaurant. The whole family must work to make the restaurant a success. Even at young ages, the children are given jobs to do. Authorities ignore child labor restrictions because they assume the family will not abuse their own children. The young children in such a family accept this responsibility. They see the hours the rest of the family puts in. No one feels sorry for these efforts. So the fact that this child puts in ten to fifteen hours a week for the business does not cause resentment despite the fact that most of his friends do not have these obligations. These children most often develop good work ethics.

However, most children do not have such experiences. Again, the children observe other children's work ethics. The children ask themselves, "How much effort do my friends devote to schoolwork? How much is expected of me?"

This issue is further complicated because many children have the idea that each subject or assignment is worth just so much of their time. They keep a mental tally of the time they put into completing the assignment and draw the line when they feel they have put in enough time.

At another level, some children believe that their talents are fixed at birth; therefore; for school, why work hard when you just do not have the needed talent? The same argument can be made for any talent, be it sports, art, music, and so on. The other position is that hard work can pay off. There are plenty of people who take the talent God gave them and, with hard work, make surprising accomplishments.

Let's give an example that you can share with your children. Stephen Curry is the NBA MVP in 2016, and at the award ceremony, he first thanked God for giving him his talent and then emphasized the hard work it takes to excel. His specialty is the three-point shot, which is twenty-nine feet and nine inches from the basket. Every day Curry takes one hundred practice three-point shots in addition to the regular team practice session. In the summer he continues this regimen most days. In 2016 he established the NBA record by making 402 three-point shots

(1, 206 points). It is not unusual for him to take seven hundred of these shots every week. It takes strength to throw a basketball that far so many times. Think of the boredom in so much repetition. Yet without this commitment, his level of productivity would rapidly decline.

This is the message of the talents gospel (Matthew 25:14–30). God wants each individual to develop his talents and not bury them. Parents need to communicate to their children that talents need to be nurtured with hard work. Below is a kernel from a Latino parent.

Kernel: **You come from poor circumstances. You live in a world where little is expected of Hispanics, and nothing is given to them. But you can and will overcome these hurdles.**

The antidote for this myth is to convince your children that there is nothing wrong with hard work. Successful people are proud of their work and haven't bought the forty-hour-workweek mentality. They put in as much time as it takes to do the job right.

Do	Don't
Please help your child to become committed.	Please don't let peers undermine your child's motivation.

Pearls of Wisdom

Kernel:	You come from poor circumstances. You live in a world where little is expected of Hispanics, and nothing is given to them. But you can and will overcome these hurdles.

This kernel is good advice for any parent reading this book.

----------------------Key Ideas----------------------

- One of your most important jobs in increasing your child's academic productivity is to recognize the many myths that deflate commitment.

- Many of these destructive myths can be eliminated by convincing your child that hard work is expected and working hard is honorable and valued and gets results.
- Children learn to be disciplined in their efforts.
- Popularity can become an excuse for children to dumb down their talents, but this is a ticket to nowhere.
- Encourage your child to hang around with the school's winners and to be a winner.

Chapter 3 Notes

1   J. Ogbu. (2003). Black American students in an affluent suburb: A study of academic disengagement. Mahwah, NJ: Lawrence Erlbaum Associates, 2003, 209.

2   S. Fordham and J. Ogbu. "Black students' success coping with the burden of 'Acting White.'" *The Urban Review* **18** (1986): 176–206.

3   J. Ogbu. (2003). *Black American students in an affluent suburb: A study of academic disengagement.* Mahwah, NJ: Lawrence Erlbaum Associates, 2003, 175.

CHAPTER 4

Rules, Routines, and Monitoring

Accomplish something that will make things better for people coming
behind you.
Anytime you have an opportunity to make a difference in this world
and you don't, then you are wasting your time on Earth.

Roberto Clemente, the first Hispanic
in the Baseball Hall of Fame

Time Marches On.

Introduction

This chapter involves the management of your children's time at home.
If you think about your children's day and add up the hours they spend
at home, you will be surprised to learn they spend more time at home
than at school. Let's take a sample day in the life of Tyrone, a fifth-grade
boy. He wakes at 7:00 a.m. He has one and a half hours to get dressed,
have his breakfast, and assemble all the things he needs for school. The
bus picks Tyrone up at 8:30 a.m. and takes fifteen minutes to arrive
at school. The school day begins at 9:00 a.m., and the day ends when
the bus arrives for the return trip at 2:30 p.m. He reaches home at 2:45
p.m. Tyrone's bedtime is 10:00 p.m. This means that Tyrone will now
spend an additional seven hours and fifteen minutes at home. His total

time in school was five and a half hours. His total time at home when he is awake is eight hours and forty-five minutes.

Furthermore, if you calculate the entire school year, Tyrone goes to school for 180 days. This means that he spends the remaining 185 days at home. Tyrone clearly spends the greatest amount of his waking hours in his home setting. Considering the whole school year, Tyrone only spends 11.8 percent of his time in school and another 1 percent being transported to and from school. He spends a little more than 87 percent of time at home under the supervision of his parents (asleep and awake). This large amount of time, much of it during the 185 days he is not in school, includes playtime and leisure TV viewing, computer use, and time with social media.

The focus of this chapter is how you can manage all of this time. We realize that much of the time is spent eating, participating in family activities, watching TV, shopping, going to movies, sports events, church, and so on. Our main concern deals with managing the eight hours and forty-five minutes your child spends awake each day at home during the school year.

To illustrate how different children spend their time while not in school, we've taken time data from one of Tyrone's neighbors, Malik. Both boys go to the same school, both are in fifth grade, and both take the same bus each day. Tyrone's day is very different from Malik's. Malik spends more time playing (one and a half hours per day vs. one hour for Tyrone) but much less time in front of the TV (one hour vs. four hours for Tyrone). Tyrone spends only 6 percent of his time at home on schoolwork, whereas Malik puts in 17 percent. Malik also reads a great deal (one hour per day). Which child do you think is among the top students in his school? Without doubt, Malik is a top student!

Let's now focus on the TV time for both children. We would urge that parents limit the amount of TV time and carefully monitor the type of shows your child is allowed to watch.

Tyrone spends four hours each day watching TV. Malik only watches TV for an hour per day. All of Tyrone's TV is leisure TV (100 percent), but Malik spends ten minutes watching the news, twenty minutes viewing a nature program, and thirty minutes (50 percent) viewing leisure TV. The news program will help him with current events, and the nature program will help him when he takes biology. Some of Malik's TV is helpful; Tyrone's is just for his entertainment.

If you are going to help your children manage their time wisely, you'll need to develop rules and routines that you can closely monitor. Let's start with rules.

Why Rules at Home?

Most children prefer their parents to have rules that provide some structure for many of their day-to-day activities. Before proceeding further, let us define the term "rule." The dictionary tells us that a rule is "a prescribed guide for conduct or action." Rules refer to the way one is supposed to do something.

Range of Rules

Few	Midpoint	Many
No rules	Limits and boundaries	Rules for
Anything goes	established	regimented
Free spirit		family behavior

At the right side of this continuum is a rigid family environment that is more like a military barracks than a home. At the left, the low end of the continuum, there are no rules, and each family member makes his or her own decisions. Chaos is bound to exist in such a home. Children are likely to have poor school performance due to the lack of structure in the home. In the middle position, family rules establish structure and limits for the children's behavior. For example, a family might limit overall TV viewing to under two hours each day and restrict the type of programming allowed for movies (no R-rated movies).

Productive families have rules for homework, studying, TV, reading that involves entertainment, peer interactions, and family leisure activities. The exceptional parents avoided the two extremes. None of their families were regimented, and not a single one of them was without rules. We placed most of the families a little to the right of the midpoint.

What Are Routines?

Routines are useful in supporting students' academic work at home. By definition, a "routine" is "a regular course of procedures, habitual." We have all developed routines we use every day. Most people have a routine for reading a newspaper. They might start with the sports section, go to the editorials, then to the comics, and finally to the main news section. We all have routines for eating and preparing meals, for shopping, for getting started each day, and for going to bed.

Kernel: **Structure everything for education first. There is a time for getting up and preparing for school as well as returning home and getting ready for bed.**

Teachers use various routines during the school day. For example, some efficient teachers establish a routine for collecting homework and another for distributing and collecting materials. Many teachers use a closing routine for every lesson that includes a final summary and follow-up with independent activities. Good teachers spend time at the beginning of the school year establishing these routines. They use routines to increase efficiency so students can do more work each day. *The point is that routines eventually become internalized as work habits.*

Kernel: **Routines must be established early and vigorously followed.**

Routines are one of the secrets of world-class athletes and their coaches. For example, most college basketball teams require every player to perform a drill of layups, where he dribbles the ball toward the basket and then banks it into the basket. The average college player takes four thousand layups during the course of the season (including practice and game layups). Another drill involves taking practice foul shots each day. Most of the better players take at least four thousand practice foul shots each season. This practice is done to internalize the needed skills so their performance becomes automatic when actually playing in a game.

Another example comes from the famous trumpet virtuoso and composer Wynton Marsalis. In his PBS presentation, he stressed the importance of having a positive work ethic and the constant need to practice every day. He reported that it takes tremendous discipline to fight the boredom that comes from practicing scales. Even though he is proficient in these skills, he still uses mind games to help him overcome this boredom.

Efficient routines are extremely useful to academic success. Homework and studying involve routines. Both can be compared to the type of practice and drills used by athletes or musicians. Let's face it, no one *likes* to shoot four thousand practice foul shots during a five-or six-month period or practice musical scales for hours each day. However, these routines are essential. Helping your child to develop routines will provide great benefits in school and later on in life.

Family Rules and Routines

Now that we have explained the need for rules and routines, we will supply rule and routine kernels that you can use. The table below summarizes the rules and routines that exceptional parents use to organize their households.

Table 4.1. Family Rules and Routines

School-Related	Technology-Related
Homework	TV
Studying	Computer
Reading	Phone
	Social media

Homework Kernels

Below are three simple rules/routines to prepare your child to do homework efficiently every day. We recommend that homework be done at the same time and place every day.

Kernel: **After school, it's a healthy snack food and juice, then homework. (Homework after refreshments.)**
Kernel: **For homework, there is a set time and a set place.**
Kernel: **Ask your child what he or she learned in school today.**

These are simple rules/routines to follow when your child arrives home from school. This strategy positions the parent to get all the news of what happened at school that day.

Kernel: **Homework is done at the kitchen table or at a desk in the bedroom.**

The kernels listed above provide structure for your child and establish a time and place for schoolwork at home. Putting these kernels into practice may be difficult at first because your children have had the luxury of doing their homework when they felt like it, but they will quickly get used to the new schedule and get down to work. The more efficient they are with this work, the more freedom they will have to go out and play with their friends. Make the time for homework an everyday affair.

Another homework strategy is to require your child to have a small assignment book to record homework assignments. Many teachers employ this routine, and if they do not, parents should. The assignment book should be accessible to you; it's not a private document like a diary. Periodically, see what work is assigned, if only to keep in touch with what is going on.

Kernel: Every night ask about homework.

As a routine, ask about your child's homework. Ask about the content—"What do you have to do?"—not just if it is done.

Studying Kernels

The second set of rules/routines involves studying. Studying could involve preparing for a test or putting in the work needed for a report or reading assignment. It could also include rereading a section in a textbook that the child found difficult or upcoming material that will be covered the next day. Eighty-eight percent of the exceptional parents set aside a distinct time for homework, and 71 percent did so for studying.

Kernel: **Make sure that your children have a designated place to work, with adequate lighting and a proper physical setting.**

Another thing to keep in mind when you select a place for studying is to keep distractions to a minimum. You should select a spot where your children will not be tempted to lose their level of concentration. Modify the studying/homework location to meet your children's optimal learning conditions. Do they study best in total quiet, or do they like some background music? Do they like to study and munch on snacks while they work? Perhaps your children's room contains too many distractions. One of the biggest distractions is watching TV or surfing the Internet.

Kernel: **Make sure that your children have the tools they need to get the job done, such as reference books and a dictionary.**

Wherever you locate the study/homework area, make sure that the books listed above are nearby.

You will find that children feel comfortable with many of these routines because they see routines effectively used by their teachers in school. Studying routines must be developed early by your child. This requires the child to learn to make decisions about what material to select for study. There is an abundance of material covered in each subject area during the year. Your child therefore has to prioritize which materials are the most important to study and really concentrate on those facts and information that he or she feels are the most critical. Since you were not in your child's classroom during the instruction, you can't make these decisions for him or her. That's why the burden of responsibility rests on your child's shoulders. However, it must be emphasized that we urge you to stay in contact with your child's teacher(s) to stay in the loop.

Here's a kernel that we got from several high-achieving children:

Kernel: **Pay close attention to the teacher, especially right before a test.**

These students learned this strategy by observing how teachers emphasized certain information. It is certainly a way to decide what material is important. Show your child that this kernel is a very efficient approach to high achievement.

Some exceptional parents organize reviews to help their child study.

Kernel: **Friday night is often set aside as a review time. The family discusses what was learned during the week and gives the opportunity for following up and for greater understanding.**

Kernel: **Reviews are done while driving in the car or riding on the subway.**

Both of these kernels utilize scheduled review routines to emphasize the important things that were learned. Both have positive results if used on a systematic basis. Such kernels also have a hidden message about how much the family values doing well in school.

Reading Kernels

Develop rules/routines for your children's leisure reading. Get them a library card when they are preschoolers. They can obtain a card as soon as they are able to write their names. Age does not matter. Most libraries have children's rooms, where there are many picture books. Many of our exceptional parents told us that you have to start the children reading as early as possible.

We get questions about when young children should start their library use. Our answer is pretty much from birth. Every US library has children's sections, and most also have parenting sections, sometimes with the former. There are now "Mommy, Daddy, and Me" books for parents with infants. There are toddler sections that contain all sorts of picture books, board books, and in most cases, computers for toddlers. Special computer games are installed for these very young children. Other sections are designed for children in grades three to five.

They contain more sophisticated books and computers with applicable software. Most libraries have very active book-report operations for children at all ages. Some libraries even have iPads for the children.

Kernel: We read together.

This is a kernel that most of the exceptional parents used; it's really a family gem.

Kernel: For young children, read to them every night before they go to sleep.

This is a revered routine that the authors of this book personally used. We vividly remember reading to our pajama-clad children who are now grown. We also remember our own parents reading to us in the same way. It's a wonderful practice that will benefit you as well. The child looks forward to this routine and learns the wonders that come from books.

TV Kernels

Another area for routines/rules involves TV. Instituting clear rules and routines that allow limited viewing prevent TV viewing from interfering with academic success. Here are some kernels from African American parents that have learned how to use TV effectively.

Kernel: Examine the TV listings; lay out the TV programs for the week, selecting the worthwhile programs.
Kernel: For TV, we select what we will watch as a family.

The ideas behind these kernels often emerged in our interviews with the parents of high-achieving children. One parent told us, "We don't put the TV on just for the sake of having it on. We go through the listings, and the children ask if they can watch this or that." This type of preplanning enables a parent to raise the quality level of the television that their children watch.

Encourage your child to watch educational programs, which promote curiosity and a sense of adventure and teach children much useful information. The Public Broadcasting Stations regularly present scientific and nature programs that are both informative and fast-paced enough to hold children's interest. Encourage your child to watch them as well as documentary programs.

Monitoring/Time Management (MTM)

As you establish rules and routines for your child, it is even more important to monitor their implementation. First, let's define what we mean by "monitoring." Monitoring means "to watch, observe, or check ... to keep track of, regulate." For example, you monitor the painters while they paint your apartment, and you keep a watchful eye on them and check on their progress. You know how many hours they spend at their work.

The figure below describes a continuum for monitoring by parents and self-monitoring by children.

Monitoring / Time Management

No monitoring	Midpoint	Heavy monitoring
Parent detached	Parent keen observer	Parent as overseer

| Child has the full responsibility for schoolwork | Parents aware of child's use of time at home | Big Brother is watching |

Decide where your own level of monitoring would fit along this continuum. Most exceptional parents position themselves either near the midpoint or slightly toward its right. Monitoring your child helps to produce higher achievement. This is an important factor for African American and Latino families. None of our exceptional parents use the "no monitoring" approach on the left. To let children have total responsibility for their schoolwork seems defensible in theory, but in practice it doesn't work out. Families that monitor on the far right do heavy monitoring that does not allow the child to be an active participant in the process of taking personal responsibility for the choices he or she makes. This overbearing stance can lead to resistance and rebellion by the child.

Rules, Routines, and Monitoring

Rules/routines/monitoring go hand in hand. You can't have one without the other. Parents that don't monitor are hoping to develop their children's sense of responsibility and independence. Unfortunately, their plans often backfire. The child simply does not work as hard and falls behind.

Exceptional parents concentrate on getting their children to work *now*. They leave independence for later. This is a defensible position based on the belief that once a child develops and establishes a foundation of good work habits and has a record of achievement, then independence can gradually be introduced.

Americans may be offering too much independence to their children too soon. Most jobs afford little independence. Workers learn to operate within a structured environment. They are required to cooperate with their fellow workers.

Monitoring Homework

Kernel: **In the early years, inspect homework.**
Kernel: **Tell your children that it is your parental responsibility to check their work daily.**

Most exceptional parents inspect their children's homework when they are in elementary school (85 percent). This practice establishes high standards in the early grades. Homework that is done hurriedly and sloppily is easily detected, and at this early age, can be upgraded, one notch at a time, until the child starts producing high-quality work. These study and homework habits will become the child's work habits later on. In later years, the parent can back off and do less and less inspecting.

Kernel: **Homework must be completed every day.**

Kernel: **For homework, there is the expectation that it is done with high quality; this is not negotiable.**

Exceptional parents require their children to finish their homework each day. They use different kernels to accomplish this goal. One told us, "I expect her to work until it is finished." This mother doesn't care how long the homework takes; she wants it completed. Other parents gave us these kernels:

Kernel: **We take homework very seriously.**

Kernel: **My daughter says I'm a pain. She frequently reminds me that I am not her teacher. However, after I collect myself and stop being a pain and overbearing, we come to a meeting of the minds with her schoolwork. You can catch more flies with honey than vinegar.**

Notice the no-nonsense approach when it comes to homework and monitoring for these parents. There is no room for argument here: the child simply has to complete the homework or studying.

Kernel: **Schoolwork comes before play.**

Kernel: **Homework must be finished before dinner; after, it's a waste of time.**

This kernel involves setting a definite time for homework to be completed each day.

Monitoring TV

Leisure TV is a major source of entertainment for adults and children. Research, however, indicates that excessive amounts of leisure TV can have negative effects on children.

Kernel: **Television, game playing, or friends are not allowed to interrupt during homework time.**

Our studies of high achievers show they watch one hour or less of TV each day. Other studies show that many children watch four to five hours of TV each day.[1] Remember—that's how much TV Tyrone watched. One of the reasons high achievers watch so little TV is because they are involved in many extracurricular activities, such as learning to play an instrument, ballet class, gymnastics, soccer, and so on. Several exceptional parents told us that "many nights the TV is not even turned on."

Kernel: **Excessive TV lowers communication and socializing skills.**

This kernel comes directly from research. Researchers found that children watching four or more hours of TV have lower levels of communication skills and poorer socializing skills.[2] This makes sense because TV viewing is a passive activity. One doesn't carry on conversations with other people during the TV program. The famous architect Frank Lloyd Wright called TV "chewing gum for the eyes."

Our society is finally examining the values that are being transmitted by TV and questioning the level of violence being portrayed. Many fear that such violence is having negative effects on children.

Some useful kernels to use regarding a child's TV viewing are:

Kernel: **No TV before homework.**

Kernel: **Restrict leisure TV if the child watches it too much.**

Some high-achieving children pick up the bad habit of excessive TV viewing, and when this occurs, the exceptional parents intercede and restrict TV viewing. The idea is to limit the damage—contain it.

Kernel: **Limit TV. If necessary, take it away.**
Kernel: **It's not how much TV, but what kind.**

Some exceptional parents had rules that allowed TV only on Friday and Saturday nights and didn't permit any TV on Sunday through Thursday nights. Others told us they monitored the types of shows their children watched.

Monitoring Computers

When the first of our parent books came out in 1995, there was no need to monitor children's use of the computer, but with the explosion of the Internet, parents have learned to be wary. There is quite a bit of unhealthy information on the Internet, and parents need to monitor how the child interacts with this material. Certainly, children need to be protected from the predators that prowl the Internet seeking victims.

Monitoring Phone Use

One thing that emerged from the study by John Ogbu was that some children can abuse the telephone and spend valuable hours just talking to their friends on the phone.[3] This excessive nonstop talk can undermine their homework and studying time and become a major distraction; therefore, parents should monitor telephone use, especially during the school week.

Social Media

Social media, in its varied forms, are an integral part of our children's world. These connections have many positive aspects and serve as an overflowing stream of valuable information. Texting has replaced the phone for many young people. However, the quality and quantity of social media use must be monitored. Parents should conduct periodic reviews of sites visited and connections made. This will help to ensure that the time devoted to social media is beneficial and for brief periods recreational.

Do	Don't
Please prepare a ***special place*** in the home for your child to store all school supplies and complete school tasks. A set place reminds the child that important school business is conducted there.	Please don't allow your children to complete school tasks unsupervised in the bedroom or in front of the television. Students must avoid distractions at all cost.
Please assure that your children have all of the ***necessary school tools*** prepacked in their book bags at night. School supplies must be on hand to complete in-school and at-home tasks. This includes homework, special projects, and important notes and letters to teachers.	Please don't wait until the morning to pack school bags and place homework in the backpack. This lack of preplanning can cause a chaotic and hectic start to the morning.
Please arrange for a ***set time*** for your child to complete school tasks, work on projects, and participate in independent reading. Clearly followed routines are critical for students to develop solid work habits and a strong work ethic.	Please don't allow your child to begin homework assignments after dinner or late into the evening. Students need to get to bed early so they are fresh in the morning.
Please make sure that your children complete their school tasks ***immediately*** when they come home, prior to getting involved in extracurricular activities.	Please don't allow your children to spend the afternoon and weekend in the house in front of the television or computer.

------------------------Key Ideas-------------------------

- Children view time as an almost infinite item, but the truth is that time is a *finite* quantity for everyone.
- Most children spend only 11.8 percent of their waking time in school. The other 87 percent is spent at home or in their neighborhood.
- Parents should develop rules at home—rules for homework, studying, and TV.
- Efficient studying routines bring better grades at any level in school.
- Carefully monitor your child's schoolwork at home.
- To allow children total responsibility for their schoolwork is defensible in theory, but in practice it doesn't work.
- Exceptional parents concentrate on getting their children to work *now*. Have your child develop a base of good work habits as a foundation. Once this foundation is established and the child has a record of achievement, then gradually introduce independence.
- Monitor TV viewing. Limit viewing to less than one hour daily.
- One way to limit TV watching is to advocate a viable alternative—reading for entertainment, becoming a regular library user.
- Monitor computer use.
- Monitor telephone use during the school week.
- Monitor texting.

Chapter 4 Notes

1   H. Walberg. "Syntheses of research on teaching." In Handbook of research on teaching (3rd ed.), edited by M. C. Wittrock. (New York: Macmillan Publishing Co., 1986), 223.
2   H. Walberg. "What promotes achievement, faith, values. and life skills in Catholic schools?" *Momentum* (May 1986): 19.
3   J. Ogbu. (2003). *Black American students in an affluent suburb: A study of academic disengagement.* Mahwah, NJ: Lawrence Erlbaum Associates, 2003, 218-249.

CHAPTER 5

How to Approach Giving Help to Your Child

I think that the only way to teach is by example, as children will more easily follow what they see you do than what you tell them to do.

Gloria Estefan

Propelling Your Child Forward

This chapter describes the kinds and amounts of help you can give your child. We summarize this idea with the terms *active parents* or *assertiveness*. Both terms refer to parents getting involved in their children's lives, either in a general way or indirectly by helping them to study, to do their homework, or to write school reports.

There are authoritarian parents in every society that use fear to control their children, and we advise against this type of control. Harsh pressure generates fear. In our international research studies, we found that excessive pressure backfires in every culture, resulting in children getting lower grades and scoring lower on tests. Our exceptional minority parents did not pressure their children to any extent. Consequently, we were not able to find any kernels for pressure in either minority community. None of the high-achieving minority parents used excessive pressure.

Pressure and support are always related in our studies. Let us explain what we mean by these terms. To isolate families that pressure their children, we secured children's agreement or disagreement with statements such as: "I'm afraid to go home with a failing mark. "When it comes to school, my parents expect the impossible." "My parents do not feel I'm doing my best in school." All of these statements suggest a demanding parent who exerts pressure to retain high levels of performance. Parents that resort to pressure do a lot of yelling. They confront their children and challenge them when they suspect their motives are designed to cut corners. This leads the children to fear their parents.

To find the level of support in families, we again got agreement or disagreement with such statements as: "My parents are satisfied if I do my best." "My parents are proud of me." These statements suggest a psychologically supportive atmosphere at home. Parents who create such an atmosphere are trying to develop a more confident child. Supportive parents trust their children. They have faith in their children's integrity and in most cases back them up in disputes. They are there for their children. The children are secure with their parents, and there is no fear at all.

One curious finding is that African American and Latino families have the highest levels of support for their children.

Why are these minority communities so supportive? Our explanation for this phenomenon is that these communities confront so many outside challenges and threats that a consensus emerges to protect the children. "Circle the wagons" is an expression that summarizes this position. Unfortunately, too much support can produce negative consequences. In one of our international studies, we found that too much support undercuts children's motivation. It is better for parents not to sympathize too much with a child's complaints about school.

Kernel: **Life is not all the time about what you feel like doing.**

The above kernel comes from a minority parent and conveys the idea that schoolwork is not likely to be what your child feels like doing.

In the long run, schoolwork can deliver more than feel-good activities. This kernel is a good example because it counters the child's complaint about having to do things in school that are not interesting.

Level of Parental Activity or Assertiveness

Low level	Midpoint	High level
Uninvolved	Concern	Hyperactive parents
Child expected to go his or her own way		
Little or no help		Helicopter parents

At the far left position, one can imagine parents who almost never get involved in their children's education. Everyone in this family goes their own way, and there is very little contact about school matters among the various family members. Each family member is on his or her own.

The middle position indicates situations where parents vary their help and activity in response to specific needs. Help is provided if the child asks for it, and the parent tends to be active for short bursts of help. The far right position involves one or both parents doing everything with and for the child. Such parents are overinvolved. This is the helicopter mother that insists on taking over everything or the father actually doing the child's science project.

In its extreme form, the helicopter parent hovers over the child whenever possible. To be fair to the parent, he or she means well. Parents resort to this behavior because they want to prevent their children from making mistakes; therefore, they insist on participating in every decision. They do not realize the suffocating nature of their hovering, but in doing so, they prevent their children from developing independence. This behavior is the reason that helicopter parents fail to become exceptional parents and shortchange their children's development.

Developmentally, it is better to encourage children to make their own decisions. Even if mistakes are made, it is better for children to figure out what works and what doesn't work. Their independence will be a prime asset in adulthood.

How Active Should Parents Be?

Where would you position yourself on this continuum? Where do you think the optimal position is? Is it best to be positioned to the far right, where you and your child do everything together?

Most minority exceptional parents are at the midpoint. None are uninvolved parents, and none of them did everything with their children. The parents who gravitate to the far left are often very negative. In the Ogbu study described in earlier chapters, many African American parents in this affluent suburban community ended up at the far left position. Here are some quotes from one of the high school students in this study:

> "They don't come home until ten o'clock … and by the time I get up to go to school, my mother's at work already."[1]

> "I see my mother on like, maybe, Monday, and I might see her … Friday night. You know what I'm sayin'? So, they are not even thinkin' of my schoolwork."[2]

You can pick up the anger in this child's description of his situation. This is the explanation he gave for never doing any homework or schoolwork that was assigned. With absolutely no supervision, this boy got even with his parents' neglect by doing poorly in school. Here is a quote from another student in that study:

> "Well, they say, 'Go to school and do good,' but really that's not enough. Anybody can tell you that. 'Go to school and do good.' But, I mean, they're never there."[3]

The problem became so difficult for these boys because they observed neighboring families where the parents took an active interest in their children's schoolwork. They not only talked the talk, but they delivered the goods by being there for their children.

The key idea is that children at all ages need to believe that you are behind them and that you are with them in their struggles and successes. Parents have told us that a child feels confident when his or her parents are involved. It's very important to show the child you care.

When Do I Help?
How Do I Help?
How Much Help Do I Give?

The three critical questions listed above are important for every parent. Parents have to consider when, how, and the quantity and quality of help to give their children.

Some parents ask us if they should do the schoolwork/homework with their children. *Our answer is an emphatic no.* One of the key things about growing up is to learn to accept responsibility. Your child can only succeed academically when he or she accepts the fundamental responsibility for learning the material that is taught in school.

Schoolwork done at home is a direct extension of school—a continuation of school. The teacher shows the children how to do something in class; the homework provides practice applying this new understanding or skill. Homework brings the school into the home.

When Do I Help?

The simplest answer is let your child tell you when he or she needs help. Let the child trigger the help.

Kernel: Offer assistance if asked.

This kernel is one of the most important in this chapter. Another kernel that we emphasize in the Don't box at the end of this chapter is below:

Kernel: Don't do their work for them.

Let us explain why we highlighted this kernel for special attention. Doing the work *for* the child at home can have disastrous consequences and can boomerang, causing more harm than good. When your children have a problem with homework, don't simply give them the answers. It is more productive to teach them how to get the answer by themselves. This approach requires them to develop new skills or new ways to find the answers. The net benefit is that their self-confidence is strengthened by the process. One parent expresses it this way:

Kernel: Teach the child how to find answers; don't give the child answers.

How Do I Help?

The help parents provide is a very delicate business. If you provide the wrong kind of help, your child could actually lose ground and get lower grades.

To illustrate, let's imagine that your children are having difficulties with long division problems. In quizzes and tests, they always get the wrong answers. You decide to help them by going over several long division homework problems with them. *Your role is basically to show them how to do each of the problems.* It is not for *you* to come up with the answers. Giving the answer interrupts learning because the child must be the one that knows how to solve these problems. You obviously know how to get the right answers, but do your children also understand? Let us give an example from overseas. A Chinese girl told me that her father never gave her the answers to her math homework problems; instead, "he gave me the solving method."

Now consider when an important math test is given by the teacher, and your children see a whole series of new division problems. They know that you invested much of your free time in helping them, so they feel pressure to get the correct answers. Despite all your help, they still can't figure out how to do these problems on their own because when they were studying with you, they never learned to analyze these problems by themselves.

During the test they are all alone. What could have helped them was to practice how to analyze these problems. This practice builds the child's confidence in solving such problems. Instead, they got into the habit of letting you, their parent, solve most of the difficult problems. This process short-circuits the child's own ability to diagnose, analyze, and eventually solve difficult problems. They have little opportunity, perhaps even less motivation, to work on them on their own. The key point in helping is knowing *how to help*.

Helping the wrong way damages the long-term relationship between parent and child. From the parent's point of view, he or she begins to suspect the child really has low levels of natural ability. After all, the parent's efforts have gone for naught. From the child's point of view, he or she concludes, "I must be pretty dumb not to do well after all of this help."

How Much Help Do I Give?

Research about the usefulness of parental help has been available since the 1980s. Many studies indicate that parental help has negative effects on children's achievement. How is this possible?

There are eight important studies with this finding[5]. Our research team uncovered the same results in four studies in China[6], Japan[7], Thailand[8], and Greece[9]. We also uncovered the same findings in studies in the United States[10].

Again, this does not make sense. How could a parent's help cause his or her child's achievement to go down? What are the explanations? There are three possible causes:

1. Lower ability on the part of children.
2. Parents helping in the wrong way.
3. Children not taking responsibility for their own learning.

1. *Lower ability on the part of children*

One explanation is that children who are doing poorly energize their parents to give extra help in an attempt to turn things around. In other words, children who have lower levels of talent are the ones that get lower grades, and this triggers the extra help. Parents in such predicaments are trying to right a sinking ship.

2. *Parents helping in the wrong way*

Our research team has done extensive interviews with hundreds of parents that tell us the real problem is they *do not know how to give help*. The help needed depends on the grade level. Middle school and high school homework and reports are much more challenging. In the early grades, most parents can help with math because the beginning math taught is known by most adults. With Latino parents, help is more of a problem because of the need to translate back and forth between English and Spanish. However, math gets harder in the later elementary grades, and it is being taught with newer methods, which makes it more difficult for parents to help without confusing their children. Realizing this, a Latino mother gave us the following kernel:

Kernel: I let him do it the way his teachers tell him because if I tell him something different, it isn't "gonna" work.

Another problem that occurs during the elementary grades is that parents understand how to solve simple math problems but lack the background to explain it to their children. For the overextended parent, the easiest solution is simply to give the child the answer. By doing so, the parent short-circuits any learning.

3. *Children not taking responsibility for their own learning*

In the final analysis, successful children must take responsibility for their own learning. Whenever children encounter hurdles in understanding a problem, they must solve it on their own. Parents should offer support and encouragement during this process, but the best advice is to teach the child to take responsibility for solving his or her own academic problems. *When children do not accept this responsibility, they look for quick fixes. If parents give in, the child will postpone facing up to the problem and, by doing so, retard his or her academic growth.*

Should You Help with School Projects?

Again, no! School projects are designed to give children depth in areas that (hopefully) interest them. Children are supposed to select a topic by themselves, do all the related work, and organize what is to be learned.

Parents frequently undermine this assignment by selecting ideas that interest *them* and then doing the project for the child. This process creates bad feelings with the teachers and may embarrass the child. When children arrive at school with their parent-developed project, the teacher usually asks the children to explain it. In many cases the child gets very confused and can't answer the simplest question about the project. It's obvious the learning process has been undercut. The teacher concludes the child didn't learn anything.

Teachers resent this type of parental involvement. How do they grade this project? There is little doubt in their minds that the father or mother is the author. What has the child really learned by this process? This teaches the child to cut corners—not to be responsible. It will not help build the child's self-concept. Many teachers complain to us about parent-constructed projects. The practice has become so rampant, it has killed the use of these projects in many schools. Rather than doing the project for the child:

Kernel: **Provide all the resources your child needs, including access to people who can answer the child's own questions.**

Grades

Usually grades trigger parental help. Low grades often have consequences. What should parents do about low grades? Many parents react by deciding to help the child, to exert pressure, or to seriously monitor the child's schoolwork at home. In chapter 6, we emphasize keeping up-to-date on what is going on in school. We recommend that you know when every test is scheduled and find out how well your child did ASAP.

Good Grades

What should you do when your child gets good grades? Most exceptional parents expect good grades, so many of them do not go overboard when the child's report card comes home. Some parents celebrate by taking the child to a favorite restaurant.

Kernel: **Every time I get good grades on my report card, my mom takes me out to Wendy's. 'Cause you get a free happy meal.**[4]

Notice the modesty of this reward. Some parents try to bribe their children into getting good grades. Some of the proposed bribes for high school students amount to large expenditures of cash. In our long experience, the modest approach is more realistic and works better because it reinforces the fact that the child's performance depends upon his or her own sense of responsibility. How often should parents give these rewards? Our answer to this question is to save them for milestones in the child's progress in school.

Poor Grades or Lower-Than-Expected Grades

There are two fundamental ways to react:

1. You can look at the problem constructively and diagnose the cause of the low grade.
2. You can see the problem as a lack of effort or motivation and act accordingly.

Diagnose and Analyze Problems Together. This practice is a very useful strategy. When the lower grade comes home, don't get angry! If you can't help getting angry, don't let it show. Instead, view the low grade as a problem that you and your child can analyze in some depth to find out why it occurred. This is what we mean by *diagnosis.* A good number of exceptional parents use this strategy. It works so well that children know their parents will not yell at them for a low grade. Instead, they know they can get help in analyzing what went wrong. This strategy puts the parent in a more constructive role. Children get the idea that their parents are really together with them in their struggles. It is important to analyze the full range of possible causes. Obviously, the child does not know this subject matter well enough.

➤ Maybe your child didn't put in enough time studying.
➤ Maybe your child just forgot that there was going to be a test that day.
➤ It could be that he or she didn't like the subject matter; maybe it's very boring.
➤ Perhaps the child feels he or she isn't good in this area.
➤ Did the child skimp on the studying time because his or her favorite TV program was being broadcast?
➤ Did your child spend too much time surfing the Internet or on Facebook?
➤ Did he or she study the wrong material?
➤ The child could have rushed through the test too quickly.
➤ Perhaps the child wanted to show the other children how smart he or she was by finishing first.

> ➢ Did the child go over his or her answers before handing in the test?
> ➢ Was he or she too careless with this test?

It is important to explore the full range of alternative explanations for the poor showing. You and your child should analyze all of these possibilities so that you can isolate the cause of the problem. Once this has been accomplished, it should prevent the child from making the same mistake over and over again. If children don't learn from their mistakes, they are forced to endure the consequences. In the long run, it's much less painful to analyze one bad experience and prevent the pain that occurs with repeated mistakes.

Lack of Effort or Motivation. Lack of motivation can result if your child has no interest in the subjects being taught at school or if he or she does not like the teacher (s). Children may believe what is being taught has *no connection* with reality. They may find it more enjoyable if they spend much of their class time talking to their friends who are equally bored. To solve this lack of motivation:

➤ The parent must spend considerable time getting at the reasons for a lack of interest in the subject(s).

➤ Can you think of any connections that this subject matter has in your life? If yes, inform the child.

➤ Let the child know that boredom occurs to some extent in every part of adult life. Children must learn to put it in perspective.

➤ Children have to do well in school even if they do not like the teachers. As an adult, they might not like their boss, but they still need the job. They must learn to get along with those in charge and show a spirit of cooperation and some degree of support.

➤ Lack of effort should be countered by letting your child know your own expectations.

➤ Emphasize what it takes in the adult world to succeed and prosper. That is what you want for your children.

Setbacks are part of any learning process. Help your child take more responsibility for his or her schoolwork.

Kernel: **If a child doesn't do well on a particular test, rather than have a punitive attitude, help your child view the poor score as a learning experience.**

Poor performances offer opportunities for parents to urge their children to assume more responsibility for their own schoolwork. Maybe they didn't take a paper or project as seriously as they should have. Maybe they overestimated their knowledge about the topic. The pain of a low grade can be avoided next time if they assume more responsibility for their own preparation and do a more careful analysis of what helps to produce a good paper or project.

Do	Don't
Please help your child to prepare for long-term projects. This pacing will help your child to be able to produce quality projects.	Please don't do their work for them.
	Please don't leave it up to children to monitor homework by themselves.

---------------------------Key Ideas-------------------------

- Parental activity can range from total passivity, when little or no contact is maintained, to total activity, where the parent and child do all schoolwork together. Exceptional parents vary their activity in response to the child's needs.
- Parents that help too much lower their child's self-concept and therefore make the child feel more helpless.
- Offer assistance in doing schoolwork/homework only if your child asks for your help.
- Supply the resources your child needs for school projects, but let your child do the project by himself or herself, asking you for help as needed.
- Diagnose the cause of a poor performance together with your child.

Chapter 5 Notes

1   J. Ogbu. (2003). Black American students in an affluent suburb: A study of academic disengagement. Mahwah, NJ: Lawrence Erlbaum Associates, 2003, 248.
2   Ibid., 249.
3   Ibid., 248.
4   Ibid., 241.
5   Desimone, L. (1999). Linking parental involvement with student achievement: Do race and income matter? *Journal of Educational Research, 93*(1), 11-30.
    Fan, X. (2001). Parental involvement and students' academic achievement: A growth modeling analysis. *The Journal of Experimental Education, 70*(1), 27-61

72

Hong, S., & Ho, H.-Z. (2005). Direct and Indirect Longitudinal Effects of Parental Involvement on Student Achievement: Second-Order Latent Growth Modeling Across Ethnic Groups. *Journal of Educational Psychology, 97*(1), 32-42

Keith, T., Keith, P., Troutman, G., Bickley, P., Trivette, P., & Singh, K. (1993). Does parental involvement affect eighth-grade student achievement? Structural analysis of national data. *School Psychology Review, 22*(3), 474-496.

Keith, T., Keith, P., Quirk, K., Cohen-Rosemthal, E., & Franzese, B. (1996). Effectss of parent involvement on achievement for students who attend school in rural America. *Journal of Research in Rural Education, 12*(2), 55-67.

McNeal, R. (1999). Parental involvement as social capital: Differential effectiveness on science achievement, truancy, and dropping out. *Social Forces, 78*(1), 117-144.

Muller, C. (1998). Gender Differences in Parental Involvement and Adolescents' Mathematics Achievement. *Sociology of Education, 71*(4), 336-356.

Sui-Chu, E. H., & Willms, J. D. (1996). Effects of parental involvement on eighth-grade achievement. *Sociology of Education, 69*(2), 126–141.

6   Campbell, J. R., & Wu, R. (1994). Gifted Chinese girls get the best mix of family processes to bolster their math achievement. *International Journal of Educational Research, 21*(7), 685-695.

7   Campbell, J. R., & Uto, Y. (1994). Educated fathers and mothers have differential effects on overseas Japanese boys' and girls' math achievement. *International Journal of Educational Research, 21*(7), 697-704.

8   Pitiyanuwat, S., & Campbell, J. R. (1994). Socio-economic status has major effects on math achievement, educational aspirations and future job expectations of elementary school children in Thailand. *International Journal of Educational Research, 21*(7), 713-738.

9   Flouris, G., Calogiannakis Hourdakis, P., Spiridakis, J., & Campbell, J. R. (1994). Tradition and socioeconomic status are Greek keys to academic success. *International Journal of Educational Research, 21*(7), 705-711.

10   Kyriakides, M. L. (2009). *Expectations for higher education attainment and press for iteracy: An analysis of parental influence on academic achievement through three decades.* (doctoral disseration), St. John's University.

CHAPTER 6

Communication

Build bridges instead of walls.

Sonia Maria Sotomayor, Associate Justice
of the Supreme Court of the United States

Introduction

Communication is one of the most essential requirements of a productive family. It is as important as providing your child with the basic necessities of food, shelter, and clothing. Establishing open and active lines of communication with children should be one of the major goals for parents. It is the glue that holds a family together.

Parents are competing for their children's attention with an overabundance of television viewing, cell phone use, social media, electronic games, extracurricular activities, staggered work schedules, long work hours, and the great distances they commute to and from work. One result is that the sacred family mealtime has been lost, which has a great impact on family communication.

Families must find a way to get back to the dinner table and engage in meaningful conversations. Many families, especially in the African American community, keep the Sunday meal sacred. This is the time that usually follows the family worshipping together on Sunday. A large meal is prepared, and the afternoon is devoted to eating and talking. It is a very special time and usually includes extended family members.

This large gathering lends itself to asking questions and deep probing by the varied family members. Personal conversations can and should follow these large group discussions.

Upside: Benefits for Improving Communication

There are many benefits to having better family communication. Research indicates that good social skills are essential to an individual's success. By working on your child's ability to communicate, you will be improving the social skills that will help him or her in all educational undertakings. It is important to be able to articulate thoughts and ideas. These skills can be nurtured and developed as a by-product of your increased conversations. Children that can communicate effectively leave positive impressions both on teachers and employers.

Communication within the family is also essential for establishing bonds with different members of the family. Productive minority families establish strong bonds with spouses, children, and extended family members. These bonds are essential for trust to develop and to give the child a sense of security. A level of honesty is implied when the child can trust the fact that his or her family has established a deep commitment.

Another benefit of family communication is the transmission of family traditions and values. Some of this dialogue summarizes beliefs that are cherished by the family. Much of it might be concerned with doing the right thing or acting in a correct manner.

One of the strengths of the African American culture is its communication skills. In Africa much culture was transmitted via an oral history that involved storytelling, which has always been cherished as an art in this community. The telling and sharing of the family lineage is critical to helping develop esteem and pride in your child's family line. Stories of the contributions of famous African American and Latinos should not be limited to Black History Month (February) or Hispanic Heritage Month (September), but need to be shared every day throughout the year.

Downside: Problems

When a family suffers from a lack of basic communication, the children are left to fend for themselves. The security provided by the family weakens, leaving the children vulnerable to forces outside the home. Many of the alcohol, drug addiction, delinquency, and unwanted pregnancy problems are due to breakdowns in family communication. Research shows that families, especially regular churchgoing families, with vibrant lines of communication are able to sidestep these huge societal problems.[1] The explanation for this finding is that such families are a counterforce to the peer culture that encourages them.

There are two levels of communication, verbal and nonverbal (gestures, body language, facial expressions). Parents must invest a great deal of time finding out the qualities that their children possess. Much of this information lies hidden and must be painstakingly uncovered by either observing the nonverbal behavior of the child or by talking with him or her. It takes years of observation and dialogue to understand your child. Much of this information comes out slowly, piecemeal, and requires the parent to put it all together bit by bit. Every child is born with a unique personality that needs to be understood. There is always a lot to learn about the child's natural gifts and liabilities.

The same process occurs for children when they try to understand their parents. They must observe their mom's expressions and gestures and listen carefully to what she says to deduce what kind of a person she is. Consequently, communication is at the very heart of relationships. It is easy to visualize the beginnings of such relationships during infancy, but this process continues all through life.

How to Communicate Effectively

It is essential that your children realize that you are someone who wants to share their thoughts, ideas, and creations. It is important that the children get the feeling that they are not alone in the world, that they are not an isolated island but are connected to the family. They belong.

It is also important that your children become convinced that you respect their thoughts and ideas. You need to show your children that you value their inner selves, with all their feelings and opinions. They need to feel comfortable that you are supportive of just who they are and they can always trust your commitment.

Kernel: **Try to understand what is underneath your child's messages.**

Go beneath the obvious and look for the deeper meaning. We recommend that parents ask as many follow-up questions as it takes to grasp the child's real problem. Such follow-up questions will give you more to work with in deducing what is really going on in school.

Reporters trying to get a story learn to ask the following questions: **who, what, why, when, where, *and* how (5 Ws and 1 H). Use any of these starters to find out your child's story. For example, maybe it is a friendship problem; therefore, start with the who question: "You seem to be upset. Is it one of your friends that has upset you?"** Parents have to understand the ups and downs of their children's academic lives and intervene before problems become unmanageable.

General Rules

John Rosemond, an expert on parenting, has written many books on this topic. He believes good family communication involves the three Cs[2]:

1. Be *commanding* (authoritative).
2. Be *concise.*
3. Be *concrete.*

- **Be commanding (authoritative).** You are in charge, and therefore what you say matters. However, be aware that there are big differences between being a demanding bully (authoritarian) and being authoritative, which simply means conveying the basic truth that you know what you are talking about. You don't want to be domineering.
- **Be concise.** Many children can get lost in long-winded explanations.
- **Be concrete.** Such messages are direct, down-to-earth, and easier to understand.

For young children it is a waste of time for parents to expect the children to understand lofty explanations about why their misbehavior is not acceptable. Even for older children, concrete examples make your message so much more understandable. Whatever you say, make sure you are delivering clear messages; be concise and to the point.

There are some general rules that govern family communication, and these are important to recognize.

Kernel: Be a communicator.

This is a key role for parents to play every day because so many other aspects of parenting depend upon it.

Kernel: Be honest. Ask questions about your children's opinions. Allow them to say what's on their minds.

Kernel: Maintain honest and open communication with your child.

The pair of kernels above requires parents to be honest both with their child and with themselves. This level of honesty is needed for the child to develop the trust that is indispensable in any sustaining relationship.

Kernel: Try to communicate on every level.

As one of our inner-city parents recommended, try to communicate on every level. Your child has needs and challenges at the physical, emotional, and psychological levels. Be attuned to each of these so that open lines of communication are established. Try to maintain contact on social levels, with academics, and on things that deal with entertainment. The more areas of commonality and contact, the more you have to communicate about.

Kernel: Be open-minded.

Kernel: The crucial thing is to talk to each other.

Another useful kernel is to be open-minded about things dealing with your child. Modern cultures are being transformed by change, and it makes sense for parents to make adjustments as their children experience many of these changes. Parents should hold firm on core issues but should learn to bend in other areas. Maybe your child's music really annoys you, but try to keep this under wraps. Maybe you feel that the different hairstyles worn by your child's friends are ugly. Teens often adhere to uniform-like dress codes that stamp out a child's individuality. However, it is better for the parent to keep such opinions to himself or herself.

Kernel: **You cannot personalize what your children say to you.**

Sometimes children will say things that they really do not understand. Statements like "I hate you" might simply be interpreted as a means to get their own way, not as a true statement of fact. Don't take them personally.

Always show your child the same level of respect that you show to adults with whom you deal. This is another instance where parents can model positive ways to communicate. Don't be surprised to see your children imitating these patterns in their own interactions with other children.

Listening Skills

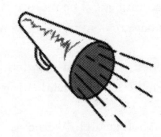

Listening is an art. Communication involves skill at being able to articulate ideas, thoughts, and feelings. Think in terms of a sender and a receiver. You send out ideas and information, and your child gives back reactions and answers to your queries. After listening to your messages and questions, your child becomes the sender with his or her own set of questions, comments, and reactions. Some of the child's dialogue can contain new information and new ideas.

Do you really hear what your child is saying? The reason for the question is that many parents simply do not listen to what their child says. School counselors frequently report that many communication problems are due to parents not listening.

Part of this problem comes from the child's not being able to articulate his or her thoughts. When this happens, a parent must be resourceful enough to spend time trying to understand what has been said and to probe deeper to find out more. Listening skills are therefore crucial. This is why a number of parents in our research studies mentioned listening as an important parental trait.

Kernel: Pick up pieces in conversation to learn what is going on.

Parents that are good communicators tell us that you have to listen carefully to your child and learn to pick up clues about what is happening. These bits and pieces of information can alert parents about things that are bothering their child. Children might not be able to say that they get flustered in class. They might not tell you about times they are embarrassed. You have to infer this by picking up on something they said that did not specifically deal with this embarrassment.

Your teenagers might hint that their math test was confusing, but what they are really saying is that they did not understand it at all. Furthermore, they were afraid to ask the teacher to help because they did not want to appear stupid. They are also embarrassed because they think all of their friends understand how to solve these math problems, and they feel left out.

Kernel: Listen to your children.

Kernel: While listening to your child, be nosy but kind.

The parent quoted above recommends listening and also being nosy. This probing is really needed to get a handle on what your child is experiencing. You need to stay on top of things and not be kept in the dark about important aspects of your child's life.

Kernel: Our children appreciate the fact that we listen to them.
Kernel: Your role as a parent is to listen, observe, and comment.

One of the parents in our inner-city studies added the idea that children appreciate their parents' listening to them. This listening recognizes the children's worth and will contribute to their level of confidence. It tells the children that you value what they are saying and how they are able to articulate their message. This also helps the children learn to trust you.

The second kernel above outlines a basic orientation for the parent at any stage of the child's development. It makes sense for toddlers as much as for teenagers. Listen carefully to your child. Observe his or her actions—what he or she is doing. Once the parent gains an insight into a problem, then the next step is to comment. Notice this kernel doesn't ask the parent to moralize or to lecture. Instead, the recommendation is just to comment and get the child to see these events in a larger context. By carefully listening, you are modeling a very useful skill that your child can learn to imitate. Children learn many important skills in this way.

In every section of this book, we have extracted messages that parents can deliver to their children. These communiqués are short, direct, and to the point. The kernel below is one of these messages:

Kernel: You can make opportunities for yourself.

One productive inner-city parent emphasized to her child that "you can view setbacks as opportunities." Many people think that much of their lives is limited by fate or chance. Some people believe that their personal disasters are really their fate or their destiny. The kernel listed above shows a parent that sees things differently. This parent wants to instill the idea that people can change things and are not trapped by their situation. This is wise advice, and we recommend it be communicated to children throughout their lives. You are rarely trapped without any possible escape. Escape is more possible for the individual who is resourceful enough to look for opportunities.

Conversation Starters

Parents need to know what to talk about with their children. Later in this chapter we include ten *conversation starters* parents can use to engage their children in meaningful dialogue. These range from what is going on at school, to their friendships, their likes and dislikes, their difficulties, and the things they enjoy. Some parents are natural conversationalists and need no help in what to say to their children, while others find talking awkward. They grope for words or remain silent much of the time.

Let us take one of these starters: "What did you learn new in school today?" Your children's answer may not be specific facts from a lesson, but a realization about one of their friends or a surprise they had about their teacher. They don't have to be earth-shattering things. The important thing is to get the talking and sharing started. Your job is to delve into your children's inner self to get to know them deeply. What makes them tick?

Another starter: "Who is your favorite character in a book or movie?" This topic exposes your children's values and interests, who their heroes are. What is it that they admire about this character? Again, the deeper you can get into your child's character, the better you can know him or her.

Another source of conversation involves sharing ideas. You should tell your children ideas that you have on your mind that make some connection to them. If you just finished reading an interesting book or have heard an interesting story, tell them about it. If something in the news piqued your interest, ask them what they think about it. Furthermore, ask about ideas that your child has been thinking about.

Kernel: **Be aware.**
Kernel: **Know what's going on; know what your children are doing in school.**
Kernel: **"Stay in their soup."**

This grouping of kernels deals with staying on top of your child's school life. This theme runs through many of the chapters of this book because it is so vital for your child's academic success.

The expression "stay in their soup" is a very poignant image because it demonstrates the level of involvement that is needed. In order to understand what your child is going through, you have to understand what his or her day is like at school. How is your child treated by teachers and other children? How does the day proceed? What subjects are taught? What is your child's favorite part of the day? What is the low point of the day?

Another way of finding things to talk about is to make sure you and your child do interesting things together—things that you both enjoy doing. They may involve going on an interesting hike or renting a movie that you both enjoy. They may be adventurous or very humdrum.

Another possibility for conversation involves finding out what interests your child and to pick up on these interests by asking the child about them. This is one of the staples of conversation. This is a sure way of getting a response, even from a child who generally does not talk much.

Kernel: **Always talk to your child; communicate about his or her future.**

Another useful thing to talk about is the future. Your child has a great many things to look forward to, and this reality means there is much to talk about. Some of the parents in our studies talked about certain colleges. The future can be centered around next week, next year, or five years from now.

Kernel: **Find out if anything is bothering your children. You have to let them know you are there for them and that you care.**

Parents are counselors part of the time, and to function in this capacity, a parent has to notice when something is bothering his or her child. It might take some probing and questioning to uncover the problem. The kernel above ends with the idea that this process lets the child know that you are in his or her corner. You are there for him or her, and your interest in solving any problems demonstrates that you care.

Another thing to talk about is to tell your child some of the difficulties that you experienced when you were growing up. What were the things that stymied you? What hurdles did you have to learn to overcome? Sharing these experiences helps the child put his or her own everyday problems in perspective. After all, if you eventually solved your problems, he or she can do the same.

When to Talk

We recommend that you communicate with your children at every opportunity. Your child should feel free to talk to you at any time. Parents must utilize all the times they are with their children to talk to them—during car rides, during meals, in the evenings, and on weekends. Suburban parents almost run chauffeur services because they drive their children to soccer practice, to the library, to a friend's house, and so on. You should use this time to communicate.

Kernel: **Make yourself available whenever your kids want to talk.**

Kernel: **Talk to your child throughout the day, throughout every activity: cooking, bathing, walking, and cleaning the house.**

Kernel: **You have to give time to your children.**

American families report a shortage of time to communicate with family members. Despite the shortage of available time, parents must find time for their children. Children really need your time. They must get the realization that their welfare is a top priority for you. If a parent isn't there for them, who will be?

When you do spend time with your children, make sure you stress the idea that you value the time that you spend with them. Let them know that your time together is important to you.

In addition to the kernels above, we also recommend that each parent spend some time every day with each child separately. Such a practice lets the child feel that he or she is special and warrants the extra attention. This is an excellent way to encourage your child to open up and divulge things in his or her life that would otherwise go unreported.

Finally, some families set aside one evening per week for family activities with their children. This could involve a game night when the family plays cards or *Monopoly* or *Risk*. Sunday is the optimal day for a game night. Scheduling family events each week leads to opportunities for communication.

Ten Conversation Starters Parents Can Use to Engage Their Child in Meaningful Conversations

1. Who is your best friend in your class? Why did you select him or her as your best friend? This question will allow you to know if, in fact, your child is making connections with classmates. It allows you to ask about the friend by name in future questions. It also allows you to begin to see the qualities your child looks for in a friend.

2. What new thing did you learn in school today? Remind your child that it is his or her job to learn something new every day. This new learning can be in the classroom, on the playground, in the cafeteria, or on his or her route to and from school. This discussion helps to activate inquiry in your child.

3. Are you having difficulty with any subject matter? Did you ask the teacher for help? This allows you to constantly monitor academic achievement or academic struggles so that you can intervene strategically when it is needed.

4. What subject is your favorite? Why? This question allows you to celebrate success with your child. It also helps you to guide your child in the direction for a career in the future. This question also helps you monitor if new struggles begin in a subject your child once loved and in which he or she was doing very well.

5. Who is your favorite character in a book you are currently reading or in a movie or from TV? This is an evaluation question that can get at some useful information. If it is a book, we recommend you read a short excerpt of the book with your child and then discuss it with him or her. If it is a movie or TV character, you might arrange opportunities to view the movie or TV program together. This can lead to meaningful communication.

6. What sports are you interested in, or how was sport practice today? It is important that your child participate in team activities. The twenty-first century workforce requires that workers be able to work collaboratively. Teams are a great way to foster this interdependence with one another.

7. What fields, in addition to sports, are you interested in working in? This questioning should be started as early as grade school. Exposing your child to many, varied workforces helps your child eagerly seek to learn about the prerequisites needed to pursue this job in the future.

8. How do you handle stressful situations? It is important that you help your child to develop coping mechanisms to handle stress. Students as early as elementary school experience stress in their daily interactions with peers and adults. Talking about

ways to handle this stress is important to ensure your child has good mental health.

9. Which app do you use most often? It is very important that you know about your children's use of technology. Learn the apps they use, especially their use of social media, and *monitor* the sites they visit.

10. What can I do to help you? Your children must believe you are their greatest supporter. Believe it, say it, and do it.

Do	Don't
Please speak to your children the way you would like them to talk.	Please don't refer to your child as "silly," "stupid," "childish," or "wrong." Such statements kill conversation.
Please repeat important messages over and over again.	Please don't use language you do not mean. For example, "Your grandmother will kill you."
Please encourage your children to talk about their fears.	Please don't hurt your child with negative body language. An angry sigh tells the child a lot.
Please ask your children how their day was. Ask what was the most exciting thing that happened today.	Please don't wait for a problem to occur to communicate with your child.

------------------------Key Ideas------------------------

- Communication is one of the most essential requirements of a productive family.
- Communication is the glue that holds a family together. Communication is at the very heart of relationships.
- Upside: Benefits for improving communication
  ✓ Families with good communication foster the development of better social skills.

- ✓ Communication is essential for family bonding.
- Downside: Problems
  - ✓ Lack of communication leads children to fend for themselves.
  - ✓ Many alcohol, drug addiction, delinquency, and unwanted pregnancy problems are essentially due to breakdowns in family communication.
- How to communicate effectively
  - ✓ Communication within the family depends upon trust.
  - ✓ A supportive atmosphere is needed for healthy parent-child communication.
  - ✓ Communication rests upon in-depth knowledge and understanding.
- General rules
  - ✓ Be a communicator.
  - ✓ A level of honesty is needed.
  - ✓ Openness is needed.
- Listening Skills
  - ✓ Do you really hear what your child is saying?
  - ✓ Listening is at the heart of all good communication.
- What to talk about
  - ✓ It is vital to know all about your child's life at school.
  - ✓ Counsel your child when he or she has problems.
- When to talk
  - ✓ At every opportunity.
  - ✓ When the child gets home from school.
- Time to talk
  - ✓ Quality time, simply put, is when your child wants time.
  - ✓ If parents aren't there for their children, who will be?

Chapter 6 Notes

1   J. R. Campbell and J. S. Beaudry. (1998). "Gender gap linked to differential socialization for high-achieving senior mathematics students." Journal of Educational Research 91(3): 142.

2   Rosemond, J. (1996). *Because I said so!* Kansas City, Kansas: Andrews and McMeel, p.60.

CHAPTER 7

Positive Home-School Connections

Education is the most powerful weapon which you can use to change the world.

Nelson Mandela

Success Depends upon Daily School Attendance and Full Participation

As the quote from the late Nelson Mandela states, education is the most powerful weapon to change the world. We know that it is our children who are the world changers. This is why it is imperative that the members of the school community work in cooperation with the family to ensure a student's success.

Your child may be attending a private school, parochial school, charter school, or the local neighborhood public school. Regardless of the type of school your child attends, a positive relationship must be developed between the home and the school. This relationship begins with the positive preschool experiences you have established in your home that help provide a solid educational foundation for formal school success.

This preschool experience gives your child a broad knowledge base of reading and math readiness skills, as well as a love for learning. When children enter school, parents must make a commitment to partnering with the teacher (remember—you are your child's first teacher) and school staff to continue to build upon the solid foundation you have established. This partnership will assist and support your child with academic assignments and encourage his or her participation in extracurricular activities.

It is imperative you remain committed to establishing and maintaining a positive working relationship with the school. Hopefully, the school embraces this philosophy. However, please be aware that not every school may be wise enough to know why this partnership is vital and have the tools in place to foster this relationship. You are the most valuable partner in your children's educational life, and you must be determined to make this positive connection a reality. Historically, African American and Latino parents have not been as engaged with the school system as they should be. It is time to change this perspective in the educational community. This chapter shares important strategies to help you accomplish this goal.

Active PTA Membership

Parents must be active members of the Parent Teacher/Parent Teacher Student Association. Paying your membership dues is important, but it is not enough. This is the official organization of parents and must be used as a vehicle to acquire knowledge as well as garner information and resources. It is also a wonderful vehicle to meet other like-minded parents. The monthly PTA meeting is the place where your voice should be heard. Advocacy for all students should be provided. According to the National PTA website, the "PTA is the largest volunteer child advocacy association in the nation."[1] The Parent Teacher Association (PTA) "reminds our country of its obligations to children and provides parents and families with a powerful voice to speak on behalf of every child while providing the best tools for parents to help their children be successful students."[2]

"PTA does not act alone. Working in cooperation with many national education, health, safety, and child advocacy groups and federal agencies, the national PTA organization collaborates on projects that benefit children and that bring valuable resources to its members."[3] The overarching purpose of the local PTA "is to make every child's potential a reality by engaging and empowering families and communities to advocate for all children."[4]

Personal Connection with the Teachers Is Crucial

As a parent or guardian, you need to connect with the teacher within the first ten days of the school year. It is impressive if this physical connection can begin on the first day of school. Progressive schools understand the importance of this and arrange for families to have the opportunity to escort their children to school on the first day so they can have a face-to-face meeting with the parents. Of course, this is not a long engaged session, and it is not intended for a full analysis to be conducted of your child's potential success with the teacher. This is an opportunity to greet each other and demonstrate your level of commitment to your child. This opportunity helps to set the stage for an open relationship throughout the year.

At one of the schools where one of the authors worked, this policy was enhanced with an evening back–to-school night conducted the week before school began. Other schools have this meeting early in the school year. During the evening session, parents and students are able to meet the new teacher, hear his or her goals for the year, and visit the classroom. This helps to alleviate the stress of the first day in finding the classroom, especially for families new to the school, and meeting the new teacher and the school administration.

Other schools invite the families to school on the Friday prior to opening day to accomplish the same connection. Students who may have had difficulty completing any summer assignment are also given support so that they can come well-prepared to the first day of school. It also gives an opportunity for the school administration to address any major concerns or logistical problems, including transportation issues, prior to the opening day. Opening day then becomes a celebration of a new year and can be entered into with great festivity and fanfare.

Ongoing, open lines of communication must be established between the school and the home. In today's twenty-first century filled with technological advances, this communication can and should include telephone connections, e-mail, social media, face time, Skype, and of course personal meetings. Text messaging has also become a very popular medium for school-home communication.

As you prepare for the first day of school, we encourage you to write a detailed letter to the teacher that addresses your child's learning style, success, challenges, dietary needs, and any medical issues that must immediately be known. This letter can be given to the teacher prior to the opening of school or definitely on the first day. The varied use of communication options should increase the opportunity for the parent and school to work together.

Many school districts have instituted computerized communication systems that share your child's grades, attendance, and class assignments.

Mandatory Attendance at Parent-Teacher Conferences

You must make it a priority to attend all parent-teacher conferences. This is nonnegotiable! Most districts mandate meetings twice a year. One meeting is usually held in the fall, and the other meeting is held in the spring. These one-to-one sessions are short in duration and dictate that the teacher disclose the full spectrum of progress or lack thereof to the parent. Report cards are traditionally distributed during these meetings, and the results shared with the parent. Due to time constraints, remediation strategies are rarely devised during this session.

Some parents leave these meetings thinking that their child is failing and there is nothing they can do to remedy the situation. It is imperative that the parent-teacher meeting is followed up within two to five days so that a specific plan of action is analyzed, formalized, and implemented.

You must attend this meeting even if your child is doing very well in school and you have not received any teacher complaints. It is a very good policy to bring your child to the meeting. Many schools encourage this so that your child is with you hearing the teachers' praise as well as areas of concern. Having your child present gives your child the opportunity to further add any insights that may be cause for concern. Your child must be a part of the strategy, so further meetings should also include your child. Please know that parent-teacher conferences must be attended until your child graduates from high school.

At the start of the school year, please share with your boss the dates for the parent-teacher conferences so that arrangements/adjustments can be made in your work schedule, and you can attend these meetings. Most school systems distribute a yearlong calendar that contains these important dates. Please review this calendar carefully to note any other dates for informational workshops being presented at the school. We urge schools to be flexible in the dates and times of workshops and presentations, with the understanding that family members are working and must be responsible to their workplaces.

Extracurricular Activities Encouraged

It is very important that you encourage and support your child in participating in extracurricular activities in school and in the community. Class plays, holiday performances, and team sports are critical times for parents to be sitting in the audience. Students take great pride in knowing they are important enough for their family (parent, grandparent, guardian) to watch them shine. Involvement in group and team activities is critical to give students the opportunity to work in teams, a very important twenty-first-century skill for the workplace. Extracurricular activities, including participation in the arts and music, help to create a balance for students, especially those who may struggle academically.

Extra Academic Support When Needed

Parents must get to know the curriculum and be able to assist their child or get the necessary help for their child. Help can and should include in-school tutorials, after-school tutoring, and in rare cases, paid private tutoring. It is the responsibility of the school to develop an academic support system for your child. Remediation specialists are available in each school, and the services should be provided to your child if needed. Please seek the support of the school if your child begins to struggle academically.

Do	Don't
Please make sure your child gets a well-rested night of sleep (eight to ten hours).	Please don't allow your child to be absent from school when he or she is not sick.
Please make sure your child has all of his or her school supplies, including daily homework.	Please don't make negative remarks about your child's teacher, school, or ability.

------------------------Key Ideas------------------------

- You must develop a positive working relationship with your child's school.
- The school's human capital needs to incorporate your talents.
- Establishing a functional working relationship with your child's teachers is critical.
- Active participation in parent-teacher conferences is a must.
- Encourage your child to participate in the school's extracurricular activities.
- Become knowledgeable about the academic support services provided by your child's school.

Chapter 7 Notes

1   http://www.pta.org/search/searchresults.cfm.
2   Ibid.
3   Ibid.
4   Ibid.

CHAPTER 8

Mainstream vs. Minority Families

Be calm. God awaits you at the door.

Gabriel García Márquez,
Author, Nobel Prize Winner

Introduction

We published our first book for parents in 1995,[1] and its focus was on the majority of American parents, not minorities. The kernels in that book, however, did include some from minority parents. We launched new studies with high-achieving African American, Latino, and Asian immigrant families. By 2006 we had collected many more kernels from minority families.[2] We then compared the kernels in the original book with the new minority kernels we collected in the ten intervening years. We found that both minority and majority families that stressed academics were rewarded with the bonus of higher achievement for their children. When comparing the original set of kernels from majority families with those from African American, Latino, and Korean minority families, we discovered a 62 percent overlap.[3] In other words, the parents of high-achieving children (majority or minority) were doing much the same thing.

Community Support Vital

The community must be an integral component in ensuring academic success. The ancient African proverb "It takes a village to raise a child" is as pertinent in 2015 as it was when it was conceived. "Community" can include extended family members, especially grandparents, next-door neighbors, and friends in the building, coworkers, the business community, and most certainly, the religious community.

The authors of this book are connected with a religious-based university (St. John's University, New York) and believe that one of the ultimate objectives for every individual is to accept responsibility for his or her own actions. God gave us free will and challenges us to develop our talents.

We welcome collaboration with religious communities. African American churches are the bulwark for progress in their communities. Historically, much of the progress for civil rights are a product of these churches. Faith and religious beliefs played a major role in the lives of African Americans during slavery. The singing of gospel songs was used as signals during the Underground Railroad and was a source of great joy and release for the slaves who worked extremely long hours, under horrendous conditions, and endured brutally inhumane treatment from vicious slave masters. Many southern African Americans learned to read and write as they studied the scriptures in the Bible during their weekly Sunday school lessons. This form of communication with a higher being was the glue that kept them strong mentally, physically, emotionally, and spiritually. It was the church in Selma, Alabama, that served as the meeting place for the civil rights movement, galvanizing the people to boycott, stage sit-ins, and march for their rights.

During the New York City teacher strike in 1968, it was the local churches that opened their doors to allow students to remain in a safe place and receive education from local teachers as parents went off to work. For African American and Latino communities, it is still this reliance on the local church that is needed today to help to transform the educational outcomes for our students and families.

These religious institutions are also committed to individual responsibility and seek to see that every child realizes his or her God-given talents. We believe that God wants parents to nurture their children and provide them with the resources that are needed for their development. That is implied in the fourth commandment, *Honor thy father and thy mother.* Children must honor their parents not only because they are responsible for bringing them into the world, but more importantly, because they nurture their development.

Clear examples of this work are in operation in cities and states across this country and need to serve as models for the nation. Some examples:

- The Greater Allen Cathedral in Queens, New York, designed and implemented a very successful preschool and a kindergarten through grade 8 program in the Allen Christian School. The schools were founded and are operated under the leadership of Rev. Elaine Flake, assistant pastor of the Allen Cathedral Church, Jamaica, New York. Rev. Floyd Flake is the pastor of the church. He is also a former congressman.
- Pastor A. R. Bernard, founder of the Christian Cultural Center, Brooklyn, New York, is also the founder of Brooklyn

Preparatory, a prekindergarten program, and the Cultural Arts Academy at Spring Creek Charter School. Pastor Bernard states these schools are "an outward expression of worship to our Lord."

- Grace Cathedral Church International, Uniondale, New York, has successfully run Sure Foundation Pre-School, providing a stellar early childhood education to students age two years nine months to age five. Students graduate in a formal ceremony in the sanctuary of the church prior to entering elementary school. Parents report that their children are well above grade level and compete in the highest-level courses upon entering high school. Bishop Robert Harris is the senior pastor of Grace Cathedral.

- Leasing of church space is a newly sanctioned school-church connection. Brooklyn Community Church, under the pastorate of Rev. Dr. Fred Lucas, leases space for Sunday worship in the auditorium of P.S. 67, Brooklyn, New York. What is significant about this rental agreement is that the church does not just use the facility; it also supports the students and staff. Principal Temecia Francis is in attendance at the service, and pastor Dr. Fred Lucas presents awards to students during the Sunday morning worship. The missionary department, under the leadership of Deacon Carol Williams and Sister Jeanette Williams, has coordinated a back-to-school campaign to secure books and supplies for the students. After the worship service, families are treated to a lavish spread of food and dessert, free of charge, hosted by members of the church.

Why do these pastor/leaders pursue this allegiance to the education of students in addition to the role they play in the spiritual lives of their parishioners? Rev. Dr. Andrea Hargett, senior pastor of the St. Matthew Community A.M.E. Church, explains that the core of the ministerial work of the church has to be in the community. The Bush administration was shrewd in recognizing the potentialities of faith-based initiatives. Schools began to partner with churches and local community centers to provide tutorial help and recreational outlets for students.

Pastor Dr. Hargett has developed a very close relationship with the neighborhood principals and works closely with the parents and the school leadership to forge supportive collaborations for the children in her congregation. She explains that at her church, she is able to use the power of the pulpit to support the educational process by presenting students with certificates for attendance at school; she also collects report cards so that she can review them and invite those students who are on target academically to a celebratory banquet for them and their parents. Pastor Hargett uses the weekly church bulletin to share educationally relevant information with parents. She also invites guest speakers, including parents from the congregation, to share their strategies for success during the worship service. Pastor Hargett believes the church is a very relevant member of the community. She concludes, and we concur, that family, community, school, and church must be integrated. Our children's lives depend on it.

School Choice (Charter Schools)

One major development in the education of minority students was the establishment of charter schools. These schools represent a major innovation by replacing public schools that have failed minority communities. The most successful ones involve parents to a much greater extent than public schools ever do. In New York City, some of the most successful charter schools (Harlem Success Academies) are housed in the same buildings as the failing public schools. Visitors are shocked to compare such schools. The public school is housed on one floor, and the charter school on the next floor. Steven Brill, in his best-seller *Class Warfare* [4] observed that the students attending the Harlem Success Academy were dressed in smart uniforms and were busy at work doing their lessons, while on the next floor, the public school classes were conducted in a much more chaotic fashion. It was obvious that these students were certainly not progressing in the same serious manner.[5]

How can these side-by-side schools (both are public) be so different? The ordinary public schools do not have thousands of families on a waiting list to attend. The Harlem Success Academies have to resort to lotteries, where only a fraction of the minority families are selected. The other families must send their children to the failing public schools.

The assumption underlying these charter schools is that the teachers, administrators, and all personnel employed have the highest expectations for the children's academic success. If teachers show any signs of not believing that the minority children are capable, they are replaced with teachers that adhere to high expectations. The public schools, with their unionized teachers, cannot replace their teachers to any great extent. The tenure system guarantees them a job for life regardless of their competence as the years pass. The charter school teachers are more challenged to perform at much higher levels.

What are the other major differences between these schools? The charter school personnel actually believe that minority children have the God-given ability to compete with the children coming from more advantaged homes. Likewise, teachers in the charter schools take for granted that when parents are asked to participate in their children's education, they will readily do so. Part of the reason for the ultimate success of these charter schools is that the parents really believe these schools will help their children get a decent education.

---------------------------**Key Ideas**--------------------------

- The children of both minority and majority families that stressed academics have higher achievement.
- Comparing kernels from minority and majority families showed a 62 percent overlap.
- Parents of high-achieving children (majority or minority) are doing much the same thing.
- The community is essential for ensuring academic success.
- We recognize the importance of religious institutions in their efforts for minorities.
- African American churches, in particular, are highlighted in our book for their leadership contributions.
- The African American churches mentioned in this book are a small sample, but they illustrate the continuing contribution being made by so many others across the United States.

Chapter 8 Notes

1   J. R. Campbell. (1995). Raising your child to be gifted: Successful parents speak! Cambridge, MA: Brookline Books, 1995.

2   J. R. Campbell, M. Verna, and J. A. Kalaboukas. "Comparing academic climates in the homes of high-achieving African American, European American, Korean American, and Latino families," paper presented at the Annual Meeting of the American Educational Research Association, San Francisco, CA., 2006.

3   Ibid., 3.

4   S. Brill. (2011). *Class warfare*. New York: Simon & Schuster, 2011, 10-18

CHAPTER 9

Notes to Educators

Introduction

The next sections of the book are written for educators, who can use the kernels contained in this book with parents, either in a course for parents or for workshops with parents. It must be emphasized that the whole book is based on sound research. Even the kernels were collected as part of qualitative research studies. We expect that educators will be especially interested in the support material that undergirds each chapter.

The *Notes to Educators* chapters first present an overview (*What Other Researchers Say*) of the related literature written by the research community on the chapter topics. The next section summarizes the findings of our own research team (*What Our Researchers Say*). On some topics there is a scarcity of research to report. In these cases the reports are brief.

Since 1985 we have been conducting cross-cultural studies, many of them international studies. Consequently, we have much to say. Many of our findings are contained in the 163 papers presented at research meetings. We also include information from articles and books written by members of our research team.

We recommend that educators read the two research summaries and secure samplings of articles from these sources. In this way educators can provide parents with more in-depth information. The *Notes to Educators* clarifies our objectives.

Some chapters contain brief sections about *How to Use the Book with Parents*. This information suggests ways to use kernels and different ideas contained in the parents' chapters.

Finally, we do not want to patronize parents reading this book. Instead, we invite them to examine the *Notes to Educators* in any depth they wish. In one of the books written for China, the publishers required us to document the different findings we reported. However, most American books for parents are not designed this way. We realize that some parents will diligently use the *Notes to Educators* source material to gain a better understanding, and we applaud them. Our ultimate goal is for parents to use the information in this book to build a sound educational foundation for their child.

Notes to Educators	Chapters						
	1	2	3	4	5	6	7
What Other Researchers Say	√	√	√	√	√	√	√
What Our Researchers Say	√	√	√	√	√	√	√
How to Use the Book with Parents	√	√			√	√	

Chapter 1 Notes to Educators

What Other Researchers Say

For decades researchers have studied the contributions that parents make. Most of this research has been done under the auspices of the schools. The schools in many instances restrict access to parents through *institutional review boards* or through other sources that monitor what information is collected. The educational establishment is busy focusing on its primary role of providing an education to a diverse population of students.

- There is consensus among educators that parents make a major contribution to their children's education. The literature on this topic is extensive (Becker & Epstein, 1982; Bradley et al., 1988; Cai et al., 1997; Cataldo, 1987; Chen, 2009; Ciriello, 1991; Coleman, 1990; Coleman & Husen, 1985; Comer, 1988; Desimone, 1999; Domina, 2005; Epstein, 1983; Fan & Chen, 2001; Fehrman et al., 1989; Freeman, 2000; Garn et al., 2010; Gecas & Schwalbe, 1986; Gorman & Balter, 1997;Grolnick, 2003; Grolnick & Ryan, 1989;Grolnick & Slowiaczek, 1994; Henderson & Berla, 1994; Heymann & Alison, 2000; Hickman et al., 1995; Hill et al, 2004; Hong & Ho, 2005; Hong et al., 2010; Hoover-Dempsey & Sandler, 1997; Jeynes, 2007, 2012; Kim et al., 2005; Lindle, 1989; Mattingly et al., 2002; Melnick, 1991; Merttens & Woods, 1994; Miedel & Reynolds, 1999; Mims, 1985; Mitiotis et al., 1999; Moles & Farris, 1997; Patrikakou & Weissberg, 1998; Pomerantz et al., 2005; Pomerantz et al., 2007; Prins & Toso, 2008; Schmitt, 1986; Schwarz et al., 1985; Shumow et al., 1996; Simon, 2000; Smith, 1989; Walberg, 1986; Williams & Sánchez, 2012; You & Nguyen, 2011).

In the sections that follow in this chapter, we summarize the contributions made by some of the authors listed above. All of these studies concluded that parents make important contributions, but the more fundamental question is how they make these contributions. In most cases the research findings are general in nature, that is, finding that higher expectations or better communication are associated with positive outcomes. Some of this theoretical work reinforces our own findings, but in some cases, our research contradicts existing literature. In these cases we highlight the differences and present our explanations.

It should be pointed out that most of this research has been done within existing school-family frameworks (parenting courses, parent volunteering, school-family communication, school-directed activities for children to do assigned homework with parents, parents participating in school governance, and community interconnections with parents) (Epstein 1983). It is our contention that these parameters restrict more imaginative research with successful parents.

- A much smaller set of researchers (Bloom, 1964, 1981, 1985; Dave, 1963; Keeves, 1975; Marjoribanks 1979, 1981; Walberg & Marjoribanks, 1976; Wolf, 1964) have conducted studies directly with successful parents. They have attempted to isolate parenting practices that account for their children's academic success.

The information derived by these researchers has been collected outside the school. As a consequence, these studies uncovered practical information that could have been disseminated to parents, but its exposure was limited to scholarly publications. This fact caused much of their work to be ignored by the educational community.

Definitions/Dimensions

Many educators refer to parental involvement as a one-dimensional construct. It has been codified by legislators in this way, but any parent knows parenting to be a complex endeavor. Like your own teaching, parental involvement is a complex, interacting mix of involvement dimensions.

We define parental involvement as multidimensional in nature (Fan, 2001; Fan & Chen, 2001; Reynolds & Clements, 2005; Sui-Chu

& Willms, 1996), where parents provide educational or motivational resources to help their children adjust to the demands of school (Pomerantz et al., 2007). Parental involvement is thus a very complex process where many parental dimensions are in play at any one time. There are more definitions in the literature. For example, Reynolds & Clements (2005, 110) define parental involvement "within the context of school-family partnerships to include behavior with or on behalf of children at home or in school, attitudes and beliefs about parenting or education, and expectations for children's future." Grolnick & Slowiaczek (1994, 237) define parents' involvement "the allocation of resources to the child's school endeavors."

Table 9.1 lists nine dimensions of parental involvement that have been heavily researched. It is a useful way to understand the complexity involved. The Epstein framework (1995) codifies the school-based dimensions (*Homework/Help, School Involvement*). Teachers should be familiar with both of them because this has been the emphasis of involvement for the past decades. Our book expands the whole understanding of parental involvement by going into depth with the seven other dimensions, which are home-based involvements.

Communication within the family is summarized in chapter 6. Chapter 2 deals with *Expectations*, while chapter 1 concerns both *Motivation* and *Providing*. Chapter 4 presents information about *Management* and *Supervision*. *Support* is presented in several chapters. Finally, Chapter 5 lays out the case for how parents should *Help* with *Homework*, in contrast to the ways schools advocate such help.

Look for parallels with your own experiences with students. Remember that parents and teachers have the same goals. They both want the children to emerge as mature, informed citizens that are able to lead successful lives and to contribute to society. Good parents also want their children to be God-fearing and lead moral lives. They want to be proud of them. Don't many teachers hope for the same achievements for their students?

Finally, we invite you to get the Ogbu (2003) book[1] to see just what happened to the privileged minority children when their parents spent so little time with them. What a tragedy.

What Our Researchers Say

Our researchers followed the path blazed by Bloom, Marjoribanks, and Walberg by isolating and extracting successful parental practices (Campbell, 1994b, 2006, 2010; Campbell et al., 2004; Campbell & Verna, 2007; Cho & Campbell, 2011; Harriel, 2002; Kalaboukas, 2005; McCarthy-Bamba, 2002; Williams-Jackson, 2002). The main difference between the studies conducted by Bloom and his colleagues and our studies is our willingness to publish our findings in outlets directly accessible to parents and educators. Our contribution, however, extends their work by packaging and disseminating useful information to a much larger audience. This book is pitched at the nuts-and-bolts level. We concentrate on the practical things that minority parents can readily use.

- Our methods are more fully explained in the following three sources: Campbell 1994a; Campbell et al., 2004; and Campbell & Verna, 2007.

This book crosses some bridges. First, it is based on years of quantitative and qualitative research. The kernels are a distillation of this research. Our research represents a bridge that connects scholarly work with the everyday world of minority parents (*theory to practice*). The second bridge provided by this book is the realization that information obtained from successful minority parents can also be used by the wider community of parents (minority and majority). Whenever parents emphasize academics, the results can be expected to be positive.

- We post ninety-two kernels, thirteen Dos, and fourteen Don'ts, and three pearls of wisdom in this book, but the book contains many more practices and messages or strategies that we extracted from exceptional minority parents. The kernels and the other quoted information originate right from the lips of these parents. These are the secrets of their successful parenting.

Each of the first eight chapters ends with a distillation of key ideas. Educators can use these overviews to clarify the material presented and also as a means of summarizing some of the ideas presented for parents.

Academic Home Climate

Sui-Chu and Willms (1996, 138) suggest that the *academic home climate* is crucial for children's academic productivity. To get a better handle on our conception of *academic home climate* research, consult these sources: Campbell, 1994b; Campbell et al., 2004; and Campbell & Verna, 2007.

Epstein [2] recommended that educators create partnerships based on a framework of collaboration, interaction, and communication with parents. She wanted schools to view students as "children" in a family-like setting. Furthermore, she believed that families should view children as "students" in a school-like home. This is the mesh idea we present in chapter 1. Other researchers offer confirmation for this conclusion (Christenson et al., 2005; Coleman, 1987; Comer, 1991; Marchant et al., 1995).

How to Use the Book with Parents
Messages to Get Across

- Remind parents that every kernel and quote in this book comes right from the lips of successful minority parents.
- The authors of this book want parents to become *exceptional parents*.
- Consistency and follow-through are needed to produce effects. It is critical to get everyone on the same page. Each family member must reinforce one another. Once something is started, it must continue until the end.
- Grandparents can be "significant others"[3] and therefore can be a potent force in the child's life. Work with them.
- This book is organized to help parents to become proactive by initiating positive parenting practices instead of just reacting to problems that occur in child-rearing.

Chapter 9 Notes

1   J. Ogbu. 2003. Black American students in an affluent suburb: A study of academic disengagement. Mahwah, NJ: Lawrence Erlbaum Associates.

2   Epstein, J. L. 1995. "School/family/community partnerships: Caring for the children we share." *The Phi Delta Kappan, 76*(9), 701–712.

3   In psychology, a significant other is any person who has great importance to an individual's life or well-being. In sociology, it describes any person or persons with a strong influence on an individual's self concept (https://en.wikipedia.org/wiki/Significant_other, 2016).

Table 9.1

Dominant Constructs Used in Parental Involvement Research

School-Based Constructs	Summarizing Related Constructs
1. Homework/Help	Controlling/Encouraging, Productive vs. Dysfunctual Ways to Help
2. School Involvement	PTO/PTA, Volunteering, Meeting and Contacting Child's Teachers

Home-Based Constructs	Summarizing Related Constructs
3. Communication	Discussion, Talking to Child
4. Expectations	Educational Aspirations, Vocational Aspirations, Grade Expectations
5. Management	Monitoring, Behavior Management, Time Management, Actively Organizing
6. Motivation	Achievement Motivation, Parent as Motivator, Learning Counselor
7. Providing	Resources, Emotional Climate, Academic Home Climate, Press for Intellectual Development, Enrichment
8. Supervision	Rules, Intervention, Restricting
9. Support	Warmth, Encouragement

Chapter 2 Notes to Educators

What Other Researchers Say

The research community has developed two measures of expectations. One determines how far the parent expects the child to extend his or her education (*educational expectations or aspirations*), and the other deals with *career expectations*. Most studies determine *educational expectations* from the children's perspective. Some parents want their children to finish college; others want them to go on to professional careers; while others are satisfied if the child completes high school; and there are some parents that have very low levels of expectations. Students that drop out of school express the lowest level of expectations. Most dropouts are minorities.

- Pomerantz et al. (2007) derived two models that explained how parents influence achievement: 1. Providing skill-related resources (cognitive skills, metacognition skills, planning, monitoring, and regulating learning processes); 2. Providing children with motivational resources (intrinsic reasons for pursuing academics, sense of control over academic performance, academic self-concepts, highlight value of school). Expectations are developed within the motivational model.

- The American Association of School Administrators (1988) recommended that parents have high expectations for their children and emphasize achievement.

- Walberg (1986), in his synthesis of a decade of studies, found consistent results for the effects of home environment on verbal achievement (thirty results), math achievement (twenty-two results), and intelligence (twenty results). In all cases, high expectations were associated with high academic achievement.

- Walberg (1984), in his review of twenty-nine studies of parent programs, reported that family participation in education was twice as predictive of students' academic success as family socioeconomic status. The fact that the family's participation made twice the impact that social class made illustrates that exceptional parents exist at every level of society.

- In reporting the results of the Chicago Child-Parent Center program (a Head Start program that continues in elementary school), Reynolds & Clements (2005) found that parental expectations had the most consistent influence on children's outcomes.
- Marjoribanks (1983) concluded that one area where families had a large impact was on children's aspirations (educational, career). Expectations encompass both types of aspirations.
- Marjoribanks (1979) reported that parental influence variables accounted for 49 percent of the variance in IQ scores and 50 percent of the achievement variance.
- In a study of early childhood students, Shea & Hanes (1977) found a significant relationship between parental expectations and reading achievement.
- Parsons et al. (1982) found that parental aspirations were related to math and science interest and achievement.
- Lee & Bowen (2006) found that parental expectations and parental involvement were significantly related to academic achievement for elementary school children.
- Parental expectations matter. This conclusion was reported by Pomerantz et al. (2005) and also by Wigfield et al. (2006).

What Our Researchers Say

In all of Campbell's national and international qualitative studies, expectations was one of the five areas that was investigated (Campbell, 1994b; Campbell & Wu, 1994; Campbell & Uto, 2004; Flouris et al., 1994; Pitiyanuwat & Campbell, 1994. The in-depth information illustrated how parents were able to actualize their expectations. Our research team collected 502 kernels. We classified these kernels into twenty-four categories. These calculations revealed the categories where the parents concentrated their efforts.

- Expectations ranked first as the most important set of kernels (Campbell, Burke, & Verna, 2004); Campbell et al., 2006). We found that parents' expectations were important for all ethnic groups and socioeconomic levels.
- In 2009 Campbell synthesized the quantitative data from 6,492 American students and was able to synthesize an expectation factor that was shown to be positively related to the children's standardized language arts and math achievement (see Kyriakides, 2009).

This expectation factor contained items that showed how parents could realize their expectations. It was a product of factor analysis and has been shown to be reliable. With this *educational expectation* factor, individual scores are generated for every child.

- In all of Campbell's national and international qualitative studies, expectations was one of the five areas that was investigated in depth (Campbell, 1994b; Campbell, Verna & Kalaboukas, 2006; Campbell & Wu, 1994; Campbell & Verna, 2007).
- Expectations as a research construct is more narrowly defined than the way parents use it. The many kernels illustrated in this chapter show the myriad ways parents transmit their expectations.

How to Use the Book with Parents
Messages to Get Across

- *Emphasize to parents the importance of having high expectations.*
- In teacher training, the experts want teachers to have high expectations for their students. Expectations are crucial to get students to put in the effort needed to learn.

- Inform parents that children sense what adults expect of them. If little is expected, little will be delivered. If much is expected, the child will work harder to reach these goals.
- Expectations contain a hidden message because they represent an adult's evaluation of the child's capabilities and talents.

Chapter 3 Notes to Educators

What Other Researchers Say

John Ogbu's research team coined the term "acting White," and in his many publications he studied African American segration in different sections of the United States (Ogbu, 1990, 1991, 1992, 1999, 2003). He was an immigrant from Nigeria and made the distinction between Africans who were brought to America "in chains" vs. African immigrants, like himeself, who came voluntarily. He made the case that the Africans that came of their own volution saw segregation through a different lens. They compared their lives with the reality back in their native countries and concluded that living in America, even with its segregation, was far better. Actually, these African immigrants prospered in America much the same as other immigrant groups.

Another theme that runs through this chapter comes from the social capital theory of James Coleman (Coleman, 1987, 1988, 1990; Coleman, & Husen, 1985). Within this theory there are the following: physical capital, which is essentially the family's wealth; human capital, which signifies the education and skills possessed by the parents; and finally social capital, which represents the willingness of parents to transmit human capital to their children.

What Our Researchers Say

Social capital involves shared values and the expectation that other members of the community will enforce or convey these values to the children in that community. Parents using their social capital want to know the parents of their children's friends. The community shares norms and exerts a degree of social control. It is expected that any adult within this community will inform the children about their obligations and, to some degree, enforce the rules. Reciprocity is expected. When a child violates the values or standards of his or her community, other adults witnessing this behavior are expected to voice their disapproval and inform the parents. These interactions reinforce the standards and norms. Social capital might involve members of the same religion. Members might attend the same schools and interact at the same social gatherings.

We believe that churchgoing African American and Latino families fit into this social capital theory. They do have shared values and socialize together, and they know the parents of their children's friends. It is within this context that we urge parents to encourage their children to form strong relationships with peers that value academics.

Chapter 4 Notes to Educators

What Other Researchers Say (national studies)

There are three studies with US national data sets that included supervision/monitoring variables to determine the effects on achievement. Fan (2001) supplied findings for students' four-year growth rate in math, reading, science, and social studies. For supervision he reported two findings where the differences were not large enough to be significant (NSD). Sui-Chu & Willms (1996) reported the same NSD finding for supervision with math achievement. However, for reading achievement, they found that supervision was associated with higher achievement. McNeal (1999) uncovered the finding that high levels of monitoring were related to lower science achievement. Summarizing the results from these national US studies, parents' supervision has mixed results.

Consequently, for most students, these variables do not seem to have strong effects on achievement. However, exceptional parents went to great lengths to tell us how they found supervision/monitoring valuable. Maybe their efforts were part of establishing a work ethic that became invisible to the children as they got older.

This is not the case, however, for national studies with parental restrictions. Two national studies reported findings about parents' restriction of their children's activities at home. In both studies, restrictions were associated with higher achievement. Muller (1998) found significant findings for both eighth- and tenth-grade boys' and girls' math achievement. Desimone (1999) found significant findings with math and reading achievement.

It is interesting to note that Muller (1998) and Sui-Chu & Willms (1996) both found that restricting the child did have significant positive effects on achievement. This finding may well support the exceptional parents' faith in these varaibles.

What Our Researchers Say

A St. John's University team of researchers replicated studies cited by Berliner (1979) with an elementary school on Long Island, New York. We collected data on the amount of time the teachers allocated (planning time) for their reading and math classes using the same instruments (Emmer, Evertson, and Anderson, 1980; Good & Brophy, 1986).

We then measured the minutes of engagement actually produced during their math and reading lessons at different times during the whole academic year. In June of that year we combined this data with the NY State ELA and math scores. That is how we determined the most and least productive teachers.

The best teachers delivered double the time in productive minutes for math and reading instruction. The less productive teachers wasted much of their class time by being poorly organized and less prepared for their lessons. The very best elementary teachers in this study spent their first week's instruction in the fall teaching their students routines that led to great efficiency later on as the school year progressed. Classes began on time and went the full length of the allotted time, with very high rates of productivity. In the least productive classes, more and more students drifted off-task as the lessons progressed until at the end of the allotted time, few students were doing what they were supposed to be doing.

Chapter 5 Notes to Educators

What Other Researchers Say

Epstein's typology summarizes the way American schools involve parents (Epstein, 1983, 1988, 1995; Epstein & Dauber, 1991; Epstein & Salinas, 1992; Epstein et al., 1995). This typology consists of the following types of involvement: Type 1. Offering parenting courses; Type 2. Communication between the home and school; Type 3. Volunteering; Type 4. Learning at home; Type 5. Involving the parents in decision making; Type 6. Collaborating with the community. Leadership from the educational community is needed for every type of involvement except Type 6.

Learning at home is often measured by the correlations between the help parents provide for homework and their students' achievement. Many studies report negative correlations for homework/help and achievement (Chen & Stevenson, 1989; Cooper, 1989; Domina, 2005; Epstein, 1983; Jeynes, 2005; Lee & Bowen, 2006; Madigan, 1994; Redding, 1992). Children that get more parental help have lower achievement. In the Chen & Stevenson cross-cultural studies, they reported that of the twenty-seven correlations between mother's help and child's achievement, twenty-four were negative, and ten of these were significant. Two of the studies listed above are national US studies (Domina, 2005; Madigan, 1994).

The Jeynes (2005) report is a meta-analysis of forty-one studies, and the Lee & Bowen (2006) study is one of the most often cited studies in the literature. All of these studies established the case that the help parents provided was dysfunctional.

The Center on Families, Communities and Children's Learning at Johns Hopkins University recognized this problem and, under the leadership of Joyce Epstein, initiated the Teachers Involve Parents in Schoolwork (TIPS) program. Epstein and Salinas (1992) provided a manual for teachers to construct homework assignments that could be used with parents. This program was implemented in thousands of schools. However, the center was not able to support the contention that this type of parental help was postively related to the students' achievement.

Lee & Bowen (2006) believed that the negative help correlations that appeared in studies could be explained as attempts by the parent to work with a child who was having academic difficulties. In other words, when there was low achievement, parents supplied more help in an attempt to rectify the problem. This was the explanation that many researchers accepted.

What Our Researchers Say

To adequately measure parental help, we synthesized a help factor that was made up of many items. This provided a reliable and valid construct to work with. If we tested children, we got their perception of the help their parents provided. If we tested parents, we got the parents' perception of the help they provided.

Using this help factor, we got both correlations with achievement and also regression beta values with achievement. Our US studies had findings similar to the ones listed above (Campbell, 1994b, 2008, 2011; Campbell et al., 2004; Campbell, & Verna, 2004; Campbell & Verna, 2007). Very often we got negative correlations between parental help and children's achievement or negative beta values of help with achievement.

The same findings were found for our international studies in China (Campbell & Wu, 1994), Japan (Campbell & Uto, 1994), Greece (Flouris et al., 1994), Thailand (Pitiyanuwat & Campbell, 1994), Cyprus (Koutsoulis & Campbell, 2001), and Germany (Campbell & Cavaliere, 2015; Campbell & Scherr, 2015; O'Connor 1997).

The international samples produced help factors from the children's, the mothers', and the fathers' perspectives. In only one of these studies did parental help produce a significant positive finding—European fathers' help was a significant predictor of their high school sons' achievement.

In this chapter we give parents more alternatives to think about. Pomerantz, et al. (2007) believed that all children needed parents to show interest in their schooling at the elementary school level and even during middle school, but as they got older, they did not need homework help in the same way. We recognized that homework changed substantially as the child proceeded from the beginning grades to the final years of high school.

It is our view that in high school, parents need to show interest in their child's homework and schooling. That is what the European fathers did in our study (Campbell & Cavaliere, 2015). In the later years, the only realistic help that a parent could give might be in the form of support and sympathy.

How to Use the Book with Parents
Messages to Get Across

- Offer assistance only when asked.
- Never give answers; make sure your child assumes responsibility for his or her own learning.
- Don't help in the wrong way.
- Get the idea across that you are interested because you care, that you sympathize with your child's struggles.

Chapter 6 Notes to Educators

What Other Researchers Say

- The American Association of School Administrators (1988) recommended that parents encourage their children to frequently discuss school events at home.

Research is periodically summarized by reviewers, and their findings synthesize reports from many studies. These summaries constitute the current state of the research on a given topic.

- Finn (1998), in an extensive review of the literature, found that parental involvement made a difference where daily discussion about school took place. Essentially, he found that communication within the family had a positive impact.
- Fan & Chen (2001), in a meta-analysis of twenty-five studies involving students (N = 133,577), found that parents' communication with children about school was positively related to achievement (r = .19). This review produced a modest but positive correlation with achievement. The talk that was reported dealt with school.
- Jeynes (2005), in a meta-analysis of forty-one studies, found a positive relationship between the parents' communication about school and their child's achievement (ES = .28). This meta-analysis derived the same positive result but used an effect size to quantify the finding. Again, the communication was about school.
- Desimone (1999), using data collected by the US government (NELS88, N = 19,386), found parent-school involvement was predictive for achievement for all ethnic and income groups.

Four kinds of communication were identified:

1. Discussion with the child about school.
2. Discussion with the child about high school.
3. Discussion with the child about post high school.
4. Discussion with the father about planning the child's high school program (Desimone, 1999).

All of these discussions were related to school or to the next level of education. The research reports listed above emphasized achievement, but family communications also influenced growth in other developmental areas.

- In an international study of high school students, Deslandes and Porvin (1999) found parent-adolescent communication to be significantly related to identity formation.

What Our Researchers Say

Even though our interview guides did not include separate sections dealing with communication within the family, our typescripts contained many instances of such dialogue (Campbell, 2008; Campbell & Verna, 2007). In fact, many of the kernels in every chapter of this book imply that significant communication occurs. Being an effective parent depends upon the formation of a close working relationship with the child. Many kernels can only be used with communication.

- In determining the most important set of kernels, we compared the number of kernels in each of the twenty-four categories and found that communications ranked third (Campbell, 2006; Campbell & Verna, 2005; Campbell et al., 2006). Parents of high achievers found communication important.

One member of our research team (Sarcona-Navarra, 2007) constructed quantitative communication scales. She derived items from a number of sources, including United States government surveys. The items were factor analyzed to produce valid and reliable communication factors.

- Sarcona-Navarra (2007) was able to find two factors—student-initiated communication and parent-initiated communication. The parent-initiated communication factor was found to be positively related to students' science achievement.
- Using these communication items, Napolitano (2008) and Wei (2008) isolated two other factors with a minority sample. The factors were labeled day-to-day communication and helicopter parents.

The day-to-day communication factor was the most important in explaining the achievement variance for the students (in language arts and math). Napolitano (2008) and Wei (2008) also isolated a helicopter parents' factor that indicated levels of dependency.

How to Use the Book with Parents
Messages to Get Across
Parents need to have open channels of communication.

They need to provide the time.
They need to be honest.
They need to be open.

Urge parents:

Not to be preachy.
Not to lecture; children resent being lectured to.

Urge parents to talk about everything:

Big and small things.
Important things and everyday things.

Chapter 7 Notes to Educators

The target audience for this work is African American and Latino parents. We selected these parents because we believe it is essential to give them tools that will help cultivate the skills they already possess and to share new strategies that will ensure their children's academic success.

Application of the strategies presented will be greatly enhanced by your partnership with the parents. It will be invaluable to these families to receive your praise for adding the kernels to their parenting repertoire.

What Other Researchers Say

Dating back to research from the 1970s, successful schools have long recognized the importance of strong leadership (Edmonds, 1979). The principal was singled out as essential. His or her strong leadership set high expectations, created a stable and orderly school, set priorities, and found the needed resources to monitor student achievement.

Subsequent research reaffirmed this conclusion (Stringfield & Teddlie, 1991; Teddlie & Stringfield, 1989 and emphasized the role of leadership. This research team found that turning a school into a highly effective one included:

1. Emergence of an instructional leader (ideally including the principal).
2. The leadership team became actively involved in hiring and evaluating teachers.
3. The leadership team often visited classrooms (visible presence).
4. Finding the resources for staff and school development.
5. Providing visible student, class, and school rewards for academic success.

What Our Researchers Say

All of these outcomes are needed for schools to function in providing an excellent education for all students. However, the success of every school really requires the support of the community. Parents must buy into the services provided by schools and must support their principals. This chapter lays out different ways that parents can support the principal and, by doing so, help the school to achieve its academic goals. We see the partnership of teachers and parents (Campbell, 2005) as a crucial element in making the school successful in its mission.

As a follow-up to this work, we hope you will journal, blog, and tweet (@docbwilliams) to share the success stories you are able to witness as a result of the application of this work.

We are confident families who employ the kernels will see a positive impact on the academic, social, and emotional development of their children.

References

Administrators, A. A. o. S. (1988). *Challenges for school leaders*. Arlington, VA: American Association of School Administrators.

Becker, H., & Epstein, J. (1982). Parent involvement: A study of teacher practices. *The Elementary School Journal, 83*, 85–103.

Berliner, D. (1979). Tempus Educare. In P. Peterson and H. Walberg (Eds.), *Research on teaching: Concepts, findings and implications*, pp.10-18. Berkeley, CA: McCutchan.

Bloom, B. S. (1964). *Stability and change of human characteristics*. New York: John Wiley.

Bloom, B. S. (1981). *All our children learning: A primer for parents, teachers and other educators*. New York: McGraw-Hill.

Bloom, B. S. (1985). *Developing talent in young people*. New York: Ballantine Books.

Bradley, R. H., Caldwell, B. M., & Rock, S. L. (1988). Home environment and school performance: A ten-year follow-up and examination of three models of environmental action. *Child Development, 59*(4), 852–867.

Brill, S. (2011). *Class warfare*. New York: Simon & Schuster.

Cai, J., Moyer, J., & Wang, N. (1997). *Parental roles in students' learning of mathematics: An exploratory study*. Paper presented at the Annual Meeting of the American Educational Research Association, Chicago, IL.

Campbell, J. R. (1994a). Developing cross-cultural/cross-national instruments: Using cross-national methods and procedures.

International Journal of Educational Research, 21(7), 675–684. doi:org.jerome.stjohns.edu:81/10.1016/0883-0355(94)90040-X.

Campbell, J. R. (1994b). Ethnic enclaves—cul-de-sacs or conduits: Differential aspirations in Greek American, Caucasian American, Latino, and Asian American neighborhoods in New York City. *International Journal of Educational Research, 21*(7), 723–734.

Campbell, J. R. (1995). *Raising your child to be gifted: Successful parents speak!* Cambridge, MA: Brookline Books.

Campbell, J. R. (2005). *Raising your child to be gifted: Successful parents speak!* (2nd ed.). Cambridge, MA: Brookline Books.

Campbell, J. R. (2006). *Parent-teacher partnerships: Maximizing parental influence.* Paper presented at the 10th Conference of the European Council for High Ability, Lahti, Finland.

Campbell, J. R. (2008). *Summarizing 25 years of quantitative/qualitative research with effective parents.* Paper presented at the Annual Meeting for the American Educational Research Association, New York, NY.

Campbell, J. R. (2010). Developing cross-cultural instruments for cross-national studies. In D. Sharpes (Ed.), *Handbook on international studies in education.* Charlotte, NC: Information Age Publishing, Inc.

Campbell, J. R. (2011). *How parents contribute towards their child's academic productivity.* Paper presented at the Annual Meeting of the American Educational Research Association, New Orleans, LA.

Campbell, J. R., & Beaudry, J. S. (1998). Gender gap linked to differential socialization for high-achieving senior mathematics students. *Journal of Educational Research* **91**(3): 142.

Campbell, J. R., Burke, M., & Verna, M. (2004). *Parental factors related to African American elementary school children's achievement in reading and math.* Paper presented at the Annual Meeting of the American Educational Research Association, San Diego, CA.

Campbell, J. R., & Cavaliere, A. (2015). *A cross-cultural study of father-son dyads with European secondary (Germany, Cyprus) and Asian elementary students (Thailand, Taiwan)*. Paper presented at the Annual Meeting of the American Educational Research Association, Chicago, IL.

Campbell, J. R., & Scherr, J. G. (2015). *A cross-cultural study of mother-daughter dyads with European secondary (Germany, Cyprus) and Asian elementary students (Thailand, Taiwan)*. Paper presented at the Annual Meeting of the American Educational Research Association, Chicago, IL.

Campbell, J. R., & Uto, Y. (1994). Educated fathers and mothers have differential effects on overseas Japanese boys' and girls' math achievement. *International Journal of Educational Research, 21*(7), 697–704.

Campbell, J. R., & Verna, M. (2004). Academic home climates across cultures. In J. R. Campbell, K. Tirri, P. Ruohotie, & H. Walberg (Eds.) *Cross-cultural research: Basic issues, dilemmas, and strategies* (pp. 27–60). Hameenlinna, Finland: Hame Polytechnic.

Campbell, J. R., & Verna, M. (2005). *Discovering the content of effective parental involvement: Parental recipes used by outstanding parents*. Paper presented at the Annual Meeting of the American Educational Research Association, Montréal, Canada.

Campbell, J. R., & Verna, M. (2007). Effective parental influence: Academic home climate linked to children's achievement. *Educational Research and Evaluation, 13*(6), 501–519.

Campbell, J. R., Verna, M., & Kalaboukas, J. A. (2006). *Comparing academic climates in the homes of high-achieving African American, European American, Korean American, and Latino families*. Paper presented at the Annual Meeting of the American Educational Research Association, San Francisco, CA, 2006.

Campbell, J. R., & Wu, R. (1994). Gifted Chinese girls get the best mix of family processes to bolster their math achievement. *International Journal of Educational Research, 21*(7), 685–695.

Cataldo, C. (1987). *Parent education for early childhood: Child-rearing concepts and program content for the student and practicing professional*. New York: Teachers College, Columbia University.

Chen, C., & Stevenson, H. (1989). Homework: A cross-cultural examination. *Child Development, 60*(3), 551–561.

Chen, H.-F. (2009). *The longitudinal factor structure of parent involvement and its impact on academic achievement: Findings from the ECLS-K dataset.* Quantitative Research Methods Ph.D., Quantitative Research Methods, /university of Denver, United States.

Cho, S., & Campbell, J. R. (2011). The differential influence of family processes on the academic achievement of the scientifically talented students in general education, and Olympians along age-related developmental stages. *Roeper Review, 33*(1), 33–45.

Christenson, S., Godber, Y., & Anderson, A. (2005). Critical issues facing families and educators. In E. Patrikakou, R. Weissberg, S. Redding, & H. J. Walberg (Eds.) *School-family partnerships for children's success* (pp. 21–39). New York: Teachers College Press.

Ciriello, M. (1991). *Parental involvement as social capital and student academic achievement.* Paper presented at the Annual Meeting of the American Educational Research Association, Chicago, IL.

Coleman, J. (1987). Social capital and the development of youth. *Momentum, 18*(4), 6–8.

Coleman, J. (1988). Social capital in the creation of human capital. *The American Journal of Sociology, 94*(Supplement), 95–120.

Coleman, J. (1990). *Foundations of social theory.* Cambridge, MA: Harvard University.

Coleman, J., & Husen, T. (1985). *Becoming adult in a changing society.* Paris: Centre for Educational Research and Innovation, Organization for Economic Co-operation and Development.

Comer, J. (1988). Educating poor minority children. *Scientific American, 259*(5), 42–48.

Comer, J. (1991). Parent participation: Fad or function. *Educational Horizons, 69*, 182–188.

Dave, R. H. (1963). *The identification and measurement of environmental process variables that are related to educational achievement.*

Ph.D. T-10342, The University of Chicago, United States, Chicago, IL.

Desimone, L. (1999). Linking parental involvement with student achievement: Do race and income matter? *Journal of Educational Research, 93*(1), 11–30. doi:10.1080/00220679909597625.

Domina, T. (2005). Leveling the home advantage: Assessing the effectiveness of parental involvement in elementary school. *Sociology of Education, 78*(233–249). doi:10.1177/003804070507800303.

Edmonds, R. (1997). "Effective schools for the urban poor." *Educational Leadership, 37* (1) 15-24.

Emmer, E. T., Evertson, C. M., & Anderson, L. M. (1980). Effective classroom management at the beginning of the school year. *The Elementary School Journal, 80*(5), 219–231.

Epstein, J. (1983) *Homework practices, achievements, and behaviors of elementary school students.* Baltimore, MD: The Johns Hopkins University Press.

Epstein, J. (1988). *Homework productivity.* Baltimore, MD: The Johns Hopkins University. (ERIC Document, ED 320674).

Epstein, J. L. (1995). School/family/community partnerships: Caring for the children we share. *The Phi Delta Kappan, 76*(9), 701–712.

Epstein, J., & Dauber, S. (1991). School programs and teacher practices of parent involvement in inner-city elementary and middle schools. *The Elementary School Journal, 91*(3), 298–305.

Epstein, J., & Salinas, K. C. 1995. *Interactive homework teachers involve parents in homework (TIPS) manual for teachers: Teachers involve parents in schoolwork (TIPS) math and science interactive homework in the elementary grades.* Baltimore, MD: The Johns Hopkins University, Center on Families, Communities, Schools and Children's Learning.

Epstein, J., Salinas, K., & Jackson, V. (1995). *TIPS Teachers involve parents in schoolwork: Manual for teachers.* Baltimore, MD: Center on Families, Communities and Children's Learning: The Johns Hopkins University.

Fan, X. (2001). Parental involvement and students' academic achievement: A growth modeling analysis. *The Journal of Experimental Education, 70*(1), 27–61. doi:10.1080/00220970109599497.

Fan, X., & Chen, M. (2001). Parent involvement and students' academic achievement: A meta-analysis. *Educational Psychology Review, 13*(1), 1–22. doi:10.1023/A:1009048817385.

Fehrman, P. G., Keith, T. Z., & Reimers, T. M. (1989). Home influence on school learning: Direct and indirect effects of parental involvement on high school grades. *Journal of Educational Research, 80*(6), 330–337.

Finn, J. D. (1998). Parental engagement that makes a difference. *Educational Leadership, 55*(8), 20–24.

Flouris, G., Calogiannakis-Hourdakis, P., Spiridakis, J., & Campbell, J. R. (1994). Tradition and socioeconomic status are Greek keys to academic success. *International Journal of Educational Research, 21*(7), 705–711. doi:org.jerome.stjohns.edu:81/10.1016/0883-0355(94)90043-4.

Fordham, S., & Ogbu, J. Black students' success coping with the burden of "Acting White." *The Urban Review* **18** (1986): 176–206.

Freeman, J. (2000). Families: The essential context for gifts and talents. In K. Heller, F. Monks, R. Sternberg, & R. Subotnik (Eds.), *International handbook of giftedness and talent* (2nd ed.) (pp. 573–585). Oxford, UK: Pergamon.

Garn, A. C., Matthews, M. S., & Jolly, J. L. (2010). Parental influences on the academic motivation of gifted students: A self-determination theory perspective. *Gifted Child Quarterly, 54*(4), 263–272. doi:10.1177/0016986210377657.

Gecas, V., & Schwalbe, M. L. (1986). Parental behavior and adolescent self-esteem. *Journal of Marriage and the Family, 48*, 37–46.

Good, T., & Brophy, J. E. (1986). School effects. In M. C. Wittrock (Ed.), *Handbook of research on teaching* (3rd ed.) (pp. 570–604). New York: Macmillan Publishing Co.

Gorman, J., & Balter, L. (1997). Culturally sensitive parent education: A critical review of quantitative research. *Review of Educational Research, 67*(3), 339–369. doi:10.3102/00346543067003339.

Grolnick, W. (2003). *The psychology of parental control: How well-meaning parenting backfires.* Hillside, NJ: Lawrence Erlbaum.

Grolnick, W., & Ryan, R. (1989). Parent styles associated with children's self-regulation and competence in school. *Journal of Educational Psychology, 81*(2), 143–154.

Grolnick, W. S., & Slowiaczek, M. L. (1994). Parents' involvement in children's schooling: A multidimensional conceptualization and motivational model. *Child Development, 65*(1), 237–252.

Harriel, G. (2002). *Parental involvement increases the academic achievement of minority students at the secondary level.* Doctoral dissertation, St. John's University.

Henderson, A., & Berla, N. (1994). *A new generation of evidence: The family is critical to student achievement.* (ERIC Document ED375968).

Heymann, S. J., & Alison, E. (2000). Low-income parents: How do working conditions affect their opportunity to help school-age children at risk? *American Educational Research Journal, 37*(4), 833–848.

Hickman, C., Greenwood, G., & Miller, D. (1995). High school parental involvement: Relationships wth achievement, grade level, SES, and gender. *Journal of Research and Development in Education, 28*, 125–134.

Hill, N., Castellino, D., Lansford, J., Nowlin, P., Dodge, K., & Bates, J. (2004). Parent-academic involvement as related to school behavior, achievement, and aspirations: Demographic variations across adolescence. *Child Development, 75*, 1491–1509.

Hong, S., & Ho, H.-Z. (2005). Direct and indirect longitudinal effects of parental involvement on student achievement: Second-order latent growth modeling across ethnic groups. *Journal of Educational Psychology, 97*(1), 32–42. doi:10.1037/0022-0663.97.1.32.

Hong, S., Yoo, S.-K., You, S., & Wu, C.-C. (2010). The reciprocal relationship between parental involvement and mathematics achievement: Autoregressive cross-lagged modeling. *The Journal of Experimental Education, 78*(4), 419–439. doi:10.1080/00220970903292926.

Hoover-Dempsey, K., & Sandler, H. (1997). Why do parents become involved in their children's education? *Review of Educational Research, 67*(1), 3–42. doi:10.3102/00346543067001003.

Jeynes, W. (2007). The relationship between parental involvement and urban secondary school student academic achievement: A meta-analysis. *Urban Education, 42*(1), 82–110.

Jeynes, W. (2012). A meta-analysis of the efficacy of different types of parental involvement programs for urban students. *Urban Education, 47*(4), 706–742. doi:10.1177/0042085912445643.

Jeynes, W. H. (2005). A meta-analysis of the relation of parental involvement to urban elementary school student academic achievement. *Urban Education, 40*(3), 237–269. doi:10.1177/0042085905274540.

Kalaboukas, J. A. 2009. *The relationship of motivation and expectations to the academic achievement of gifted Korean American students.* Doctoral disseration, St. John's University.

Keeves, J. P. (1975). The home the school and achievement in mathematics and science. *Science Education, 59*, 439–460.

Keith, T., Keith, P., Quirk, K., Cohen-Rosemthal, E., & Franzese, B. (1996). Effectss of parent involvement on achievement for students who attend school in rural America. *Journal of Research in Rural Education, 12*(2), 55-67.

Keith, T., Keith, P., Troutman, G., Bickley, P., Trivette, P., & Singh, K. (1993). Does parental involvement affect eighth-grade student achievement? Structural analysis of national data. *School Psychology Review, 22*(3), 474-496.

Kim, J., Murdock, T., & Choi, J. (2005). Investigation of parents' beliefs about readiness for kindergarten: An examination of National Household Education Survey (NHES:93). *Educational Research Quarterly, 29*(2), 3–18.

Koutsoulis, M., & Campbell, J. R. (2001). Family processes affect students' motivation, science, and math achievement in Cypriot high schools. *Structural Equation Modeling, 8*(1), 108–127.

Kyriakides, M. L. (2009). *Expectations for higher education attainment and press for iteracy: An analysis of parental influence on academic achievement through three decades.* Doctoral disseration, St. John's University.

Lee, J.-S., & Bowen, N. K. (2006). Parent involvement, cultural capital, and the achievement gap among elementary school children. *American Educational Research Journal, 43*(2), 193–218. doi:10.3102/00028312043002193.

Lindle, J. (1989). What do parents want from principals and teachers? *Educational Leadership, 47*(2), 12–14.

Madigan, T. (1994). *Parent involvement and school achievement.* Paper presented at the Annual Meeting of the American Educational Research Association, New Orleans, LA.

Marchant, G., Paulson, S., & Rothlisberg, B. (1995). *Parents perceptions of teacher outreach and parent involvement in children's education.* Paper presented at the Annual Meeting of the American Educational Research Association.

Marjoribanks, K. (1979). Family environments. In H. Walberg (Ed.), *Educational environments and effects* (pp. 15–37). Beverly, CA: McCutchan Publishing Corp.

Marjoribanks, K. (1981). Family environments and children's academic achievement. Sex and social group differences. *Journal of Psychology, 109,* 155–164.

Marjoribanks, K. (1983). Social class, environments and adolescents' aspirations. *Educational Studies, 9*(3), 135–143. doi:10.3102/00346543067003339.

Mattingly, D., Prislin, R., McKenzie, J., Rodriquez, J., & Kayzar, B. (2002). Evaluating evaluations: The case of parent involvement programs. *Review of Educational Research, 72*(4), 549–576. doi:10.3102/00346543072004549.

McCarthy-Bamba, P. (2002). *The telling of stories: A parental involvement strategy for improving/motivating student achievement outcomes in African America.* Doctoral dissertation, St. John's University.

McNeal, R. (1999). Parental involvement as social capital: Differential effectiveness on science achievement, truancy, and dropping out. *Social Forces, 78*(1), 117–144.

Melnick, C. R. (1991). Parents and teachers as educative partners. *International Journal of Educational Research,* *15*(2), 125–227. doi:http://dx.doi.org.jerome.stjohns.edu:81/10.1016/0883-0355(91)90029-R.

Merttens, R., & Woods, P. (1994). *Parents' and childrens' assessment of maths at home: Toward a theory of learning congruences.* Paper presented at the Annual Meeting of the American Educational Research Association, New Orleans, LA.

Miedel, W., & Reynolds, A. J. (1999). Parent involvement in early intervention for disadvantaged children: Does it matter? *Journal of School Psychology, 37*(4), 379–402. doi:http://dx.doi.org.jerome.stjohns.edu:81/10.1016/S0022-4405(99)00023-0.

Mims, G. L. (1985). Aspiration, expectation, and parental influences among upward bound students in three institutions. *Educational and Psychological Research, 5*(3), 181–190.

Mitiotis, D., Sesma, A., & Masten, A. (1999). Parenting as a protective process for school success in children from homeless families. *Early Education and Development, 10*(2), 111–133. doi:10.1207/s15566935eed1002_2.

Moles, O., & Farris, E. (1997). *Social communication with families: A national perspective.* Paper presented at the annual meeting of the American Educational Research Association, Chicago, IL.

Muller, C. (1998). Gender differences in parental involvement and adolescents' mathematics achievement. *Sociology of Education, 71*(4), 336–356.

Napolitano, R. (2008). *The effects of parental involvement in middle schools: Schools Under Register Review (SURR) vs. schools in good standing.* Doctoral dissertation, St. John's University.

O'Connor, S. (1997). *The linkages among the home environment and academic self-concepts on achievement of contemporary family structures of German high school students.* (doctoral disseration), St. John's University.

Ogbu, J. (1991). Low school performance as an adaptation: The case of Blacks in Stockton, California. In M. Gibson & J. Ogbu (Eds.), pp. 249-285 *Minority status and schooling: A comparative study of immigrant and involuntary minorities*. New York: Garland Publishing, Inc.

Ogbu, J. (1999). *The significance of minority status*. Paper presented at the Annual Meeting of the American Educational Research Association, Montreal, Canada.

Ogbu, J. (2003). *Black American students in an affluent suburb: A study of academic disengagement*. Mahwah, NJ: Lawrence Erlbaum Associates.

Ogbu, J. U. (1990). Understanding diversity: Summary comments. *Education and Urban Society, 22*(4), 425–429.

Ogbu, J. U. (1992). Adaptation to minority status and impact on school success. *Theory into Practice 31*(4), 287-294.

Parsons, J., Kaczala, C., & Meece, J. (1982). Socialization of achievement attitudes and beliefs: Classroom influences. *Child Development, 53*, 322–339.

Patrikakou, E., & Weissberg, R. (1998). *Parents' perceptions of teacher outreach and parent involvement in children's education.* Paper presented at the Annual Meeting of the American Educational Research Association, San Diego, CA.

Pitiyanuwat, S., & Campbell, J. R. (1994). Socio-economic status has major effects on math achievement, educational aspirations and future job expectations of elementary school children in Thailand. *International Journal of Educational Research, 21*(7), 713–738.

Pomerantz, E., Grolnick, W., & Price, C. (2005). The role of parents in how children approach school: A dynamic perspective." In A. J. Elliot & C. S. Dweck (Eds.), *The handbook of competence and motivation* (259–278). New York: Guilford.

Pomerantz, E., Moorman, E., & Litwack, S. (2007). The how, whom, and why of parents' involvement in children's academic lives: More is not always better. *Review of Educational Research, 77*(3), 373–410. doi:10.3102/003465430305567.

Prins, E., & Toso, B. (2008). Defining and measuring parenting for educational success: A critical discourse analysis of the parent education profile. *American Education Research Journal, 45*(3), 555–596. doi:10.3102/0002831208316205.

Redding, S. (1992). *Parent scale to measure the efficacy of strategies to enhance the curriculum of the home.* Paper presented at the Annual Meeting of the American Educational Research Association, San Francisco, CA.

Reynolds, A., & Clements, M. (2005). Parental involvement and children's school success. In E. Patrikakou, R. Weissberg, S. Redding, & H. J. Walberg (Eds.), *School-family partnerships for children's success* (pp. 109–127). New York: Teachers College Press.

Rosemond, J. (1996). *Because I said so!* Kansas City, Kansas: Andrews and McMeel.

Sarcona-Navarra, M. (2007). *The effects of parental involvement on achievement and motivation in science for high school students.* Doctoral disseration, St. John's University.

Schmitt, D. (1986). Parents and schools as partners in preschool education. *Educational Leadership, 44*(3), 40–41.

Schwarz, J., Barton-Henry, M., & Pruzinsky, T. 1985. Assessing childrearing behaviors: A comparison of ratings made by mother, father, child and sibling on the CRPBI. *Child Development, 56,* 462–479.

Shea, J. J., & Hanes, M. L. (1977). *The relationship between measures of home environment and school achievement of follow through children.* Paper presented at the Annual Meeting of the American Educational Research Association, New York, NY.

Shumow, L., Vandell, D., & Kang, K. (1996). School choice, family characteristics and home-school relations: Contributions to school achievement. *Journal of Educational Policy, 88*(3), 451–460.

Simon, B. (2000). *Predictors of high school and family partnerships and the influence of partnerships on student success.* The John's Hopkins University, Baltimore, MD.

Smith, T. E. (1989). Mother-father differences in parental influence on school grades and educational goals. *Sociological Inquiry, 59,* 88–98.

Stringfield, S., & Teddlie, C. (1991). Observers as Predictors of Schools' Multiyear Outlier Status on Achievement Tests. *The Elementary School Journal, 91*(4), 357-376.

Sui-Chu, E. H., & Willms, J. D. (1996). Effects of parental involvement on eighth-grade achievement. *Sociology of Education, 69*(2), 126–141.

Teddlie, C., Kirby, P. C., & Stringfield, S. (1989). Effective versus ineffective schools: Observable differences in the classroom. *American Journal of Education, 97*(3), 221–236.

Walberg, H. (1984). Families as partners in educational productivity. *Phi Delta Kappan, 65*(6), 397–400.

Walberg, H. (1986). "Syntheses of research on teaching." In M. C. Wittrock (Ed.), *Handbook of research on teaching* (3rd ed.) (pp. 214–229). (New York: Macmillan Publishing Co.)

Walberg, H. (May 1986). What promotes achievement, faith, values, and life skills in Catholic schools? *Momentum* (May 1986): 19.

Walberg, H. J., & Marjoribanks, K. (1976). Family environment and cognitive development: Twelve analytic models." *Review of Educational Research, 46,* 527–551.

Wei, D. (2008). *Perceptions of family processes and the effects on middle school students' achievement.* Ed.D. 3347090, St. John's University, New York, School of Education and Human Services.

Wigfield, A., Eccles, J., Schiefele, U., Roeser, R., & Davis-Kean, P. (2006). Development of achievement motivation. In N. Eisenberg (Ed.), *Handbook of child psychology: Vol. 3 Social, emotional, and personality development* (6th ed.) pp.933-1002. Hoboken, NJ: John Wiley.

Williams, T. T., & Sánchez, B. (2012). Parental involvement (and uninvolvement) at an inner-city high school. *Urban Education, 47*(3), 625–652. doi:10.1177/0042085912437794.

Williams-Jackson, B. (2002). *Parental involvement: An essential ingredient in improving student academic outcomes.* Doctoral disseration, St. John's University.

Wolf, R. M. (1964). *The identification and measurement of environmental process variables related to intelligence.* Doctoral dissertation, University of Chicago.

You, S., & Nguyen, J. T. (2011). Parents' involvement in adolescents' schooling: A multidimensional conceptualisation and mediational model. *Educational Psychology, 31*(5), 547–558. do i:10.1080/01443410.2011.577734.

APPENDIX

Chapter 2

Kernel	Quality time, simply put, is when your child wants time.
Kernel	Quality time is important. Even with a busy schedule, take the time to show him or her that you care.
Kernel	Education is the key to a successful life.
Kernel	My son knows how I feel about education because I am like a broken record every time I remind him that our ancestors fought and died for the right to go to school and to get a good education.
Kernel	I expect my child to view school as important.
Kernel	Without education you can't go anywhere.
Kernel	Education is what matters.
Kernel	I just want my children to realize their potential and not to be afraid of it.
Kernel	Education is food for the mind.
Kernel	Education gives you life skills.
Kernel	We have to do handwork to make hard money. If our child gets an education, he or she will get that opportunity. That will be like breaking the chain, and that will benefit my pride. I'd be proud of my children if they became construction workers, but I would love for them to get a little piece of paper that says they're a "this."

Kernel	Value education by saying it so often that your child believes it.
Kernel	Whatever you are, you must be the best at it.
Kernel	He knows that we work so that he can have a better life.
Kernel	I want my daughter to be more than I am.
Kernel	Education is the inheritance that we are going to give them for their whole lives.
Kernel	It's not where you come from; it's where you are going.
Kernel	Education is the ticket to the future.
Kernel	Effort is necessary for ability to show.
Kernel	Ability without effort goes nowhere.
Kernel	Ability is what God gave you; effort makes you grow.
Kernel	Achievement depends upon effort.
Kernel	If there are children that get one hundred, my child has to get one hundred.
Kernel	Success is based upon the foundation of hard work, honesty, flexibility, dependability, adaptability, being well-read, and being well-spoken.
Kernel	If you want good, your nose has to run.
Kernel	Make your liability your asset.
Kernel	Your job is school.

Chapter 3

Kernel	Have your children bring their friends home; know their friends.
Kernel	Let your house be the home that your children's friends all gather at because, if you know their friends, it reveals something very important about your own children.
Kernel	Get to know your children's friends' parents.

Kernel	Look at your children's buddy list on the computer. Know what they are doing and with whom they are chatting.
Kernel	You come from poor circumstances. You live in a world where little is expected of Hispanics, and nothing is given to them. But you can and will overcome these hurdles.

Chapter 4

Kernel	Structure everything for education first. There is a time for getting up and preparing for school as well as returning home and getting ready for bed.
Kernel	Routines must be established early and vigorously followed.
Kernel	After school, it's a healthy snack food and juice, then homework. (Homework after refreshments.)
Kernel	For homework, there is a set time and a set place.
Kernel	Ask your child what he or she learned in school today.
Kernel	Homework is done at the kitchen table or at a desk in the bedroom.
Kernel	Every night ask about homework.
Kernel	Make sure that your children have a designated place to work, with adequate lighting and a proper physical setting.
Kernel	Make sure that your children have the tools they need to get the job done, such as reference books and a dictionary.
Kernel	Pay close attention to the teacher, especially right before a test.

Kernel	Friday night is often set aside as a review time. The family discusses what was learned during the week and gives the opportunity for following up and for greater understanding.
Kernel	Reviews are done while driving in the car or riding on the subway.
Kernel	We read together.
Kernel	For young children, read to them every night before they go to sleep.
Kernel	Examine the TV listings; lay out the TV programs for the week, selecting the worthwhile programs.
Kernel	For TV, we select what we will watch as a family.
Kernel	In the early years, inspect homework.
Kernel	Tell your children that it is your parental responsibility to check their work daily.
Kernel	Homework must be completed every day.
Kernel	For homework, there is the expectation that it is done with high quality; this is not negotiable.

Chapter 4 Continued

Kernel	We take homework very seriously.
Kernel	My daughter says I'm a pain. She frequently reminds me that I am not her teacher. However, after I collect myself and stop being a pain and overbearing, we come to a meeting of the minds with her schoolwork. You can catch more flies with honey than vinegar.
Kernel	Schoolwork comes before play.
Kernel	Homework must be finished before dinner; after, it's a waste of time.
Kernel	Television, game playing, or friends are not allowed to interrupt during homework time.

Kernel	Excessive TV lowers communication and socializing skills.
Kernel	No TV before homework.
Kernel	Restrict leisure TV if the child watches it too much.
Kernel	Limit TV. If necessary, take it away.
Kernel	It's not how much TV, but what kind.

Chapter 5

Kernel	Life is not all the time about what you feel like doing.
Kernel	Offer assistance if asked.
Kernel	Don't do their work for them.
Kernel	Teach the child how to find *answers*; *don't* give the child answers.
Kernel	I let him do it the way his teachers tell him because if I tell him something different, it isn't "gonna" work.
Kernel	Provide all the resources your child needs, including access to people who can answer the child's own questions.
Kernel	Every time I get good grades on my report card, my mom takes me out to Wendy's. 'Cause you get a free happy meal.
Kernel	If a child doesn't do well on a particular test, rather than have a punitive attitude, help your child view the poor score as a learning experience.

Chapter 6

Kernel	Try to understand what is underneath your child's messages.
Kernel	Be a communicator.
Kernel	Be honest. Ask questions about your children's opinions. Allow them to say what's on their minds.

Kernel	Maintain honest and open communication with your child.
Kernel	Try to communicate on every level.
Kernel	Be open-minded.
Kernel	The crucial thing is to talk to each other.
Kernel	You cannot personalize what your children say to you.
Kernel	Pick up pieces in conversation to learn what is going on.
Kernel	Listen to your children.
Kernel	While listening to your child, be nosy but kind.
Kernel	Our children appreciate the fact that we listen to them.
Kernel	Your role as a parent is to listen, observe, and comment.
Kernel	You can make opportunities for yourself.
Kernel	Be aware.
Kernel	Know what's going on; know what your children are doing in school.
Kernel	"Stay in their soup."
Kernel	Always talk to your child; communicate about his or her future.
Kernel	Find out if anything is bothering your children. You have to let them know you are there for them and that you care.
Kernel	Make yourself available whenever your kids want to talk.
Kernel	Talk to your child throughout the day, throughout every activity: cooking, bathing, walking, and cleaning the house.
Kernel	You have to give time to your children.